TOW TRUCKS

A PHOTOGRAPHIC HISTORY

RARE FIND OUTSIDE of the U.S.A

JOHN GUNNELL AND TOM COLLINS

Published by

 krause publications
An F+W Publications Company

700 East State Street • Iola, WI 54990-0001
715-445-2214 • 888-457-2873
www.krause.com

Please, call or write us for our free catalog of publications.
Our toll-free number to place an order or obtain a free catalog is 800-258-0929
or please us our regular business telephone 715-445-2214.

ISBN: 0-87349-582-9
Library of Congress Number: 2002113133
Printed in the United States of America

Edited by Tom Collins
Designed by Brian Brogaard

ACKNOWLEDGMENTS

HELPFUL TOW PROFESSIONALS:

Al Barcelow
Hap Cramer
Bob Dearth
Kingsley Foreman
Bob Gary
Bob Gilder
Patrick Gilliam
Adrian and Terry Goodrich
Nathan Kenworthy
Todd Klismet
Pete Laurie
Jay Lorenz
Donal Loker

Mike Markesich
Bill Middleton
Phillip Morrison
Doug Nye
Vern O'Brien
Bill Oaks
Randy Olson
Betty and Darrell Parnham
Albert Sawallich
John Stuppy
Henry Vanden Heuvel
Earl Youngberg
Tim and Jennie Rudolph

RESTORERS AND ENTHUSIASTS:

Gilbert Alpers
Bill Berg
Charles Betz
Bruce Craig
James Degnan
Gil Delgado
Don Dugal
Joe Egle
Brian Furman
Ken Goudy
Jim Gustafson
John Hanson
Roger Heinbach
Phillip Hubbard

Robert Loudon
Alan Merkel
Don Metzler
John Murray
Dave Netherland
Bruce Palmer
Terry Patton
Bob Pierce
Mark Redman
Richard Sorrels
Joe Stout
Coy Thomas
Ken Voigt
Mark Wayman

SPECIAL THANKS

Buena Vista County Journal (Iowa), Dale Garlock, editor
Bill Candler, Towing and Recovery News
Dixie Industries
Ebersole Pontiac, Buick, Honda and GMC, Randy Ebersole
Green Flag (United Kingdom), Melanie Denny, media relations
Hagerty Insurance, Sydney McManus

and Corey Seefeldt, media relations
Indianapolis Motor Speedway
International Towing and Recovery Museum
Jerr Dan Lift
Earl Johnson/ Lotus Productions
Ron Kowalke, Old Cars Weekly
Labatt Brewing Co. Ltd., Nellie Swart, archives
Lanser Towing
Mack Truck Historical Archives

On Mark, International
PATH (Port Authority of New York), Tim Thompson
Precision Frame Inc.
Revell Models
Jack Sheridan and the family of Kemp Olson
Smith Miller Toys Inc.
Angelo Van Bogart, Old Cars Weekly
Weld-Built Wreckers and Carriers

Footnotes: Towing and Recovery News

ABOUT THE AUTHORS

JOHN GUNNELL

One might say John Gunnell has an eye for cars and trucks. At one time, he dedicated his education to becoming an automotive designer. But he also wanted to tell stories of the industry and soon was painting images through the printed word. John has become an authoritative source of automotive information during his 25-year career that has included writing articles for a variety of publications, editing Old Cars Weekly and authoring countless books. He is an avid collector of automobiles and automobilia and has taught college level classes. John explores all topics automotive with a zest that invites readers to come along on the journey with him. He lives in Iola, Wisconsin, and is an author in residence with Krause Publications.

TOM COLLINS

While new to the world of automotive publishing, Tom Collins has been an automotive hobbyist most of his life. He has worked in broadcasting, media relations, corporate communications and video documentary production over his 27-year career. A former media relations assistant with the Green Bay Packers, Tom enjoyed researching, writing and producing two syndicated television series about the Packers and the N.F.L. He authored a book about the Green Bay Packers Hall of Fame. Tom has collected scale model cars and trucks and automotive literature since his childhood. His style is to bring out the personal stories of people like the tow truck drivers and collectors found in this book.

CONTENTS

INTRODUCTION

There's something unique about a tow truck heading down a highway or rolling across a city street. Tow trucks are unique-looking vehicles that turn heads as they travel to their mission of service.

Just as the trucks are unique, so are their drivers, men and women who quietly dedicate their lives to rescuing injured people from damaged vehicles, clearing highways that have been littered with accident debris, hauling disabled vehicles in for repair and doing all kinds of heavy lifting.

Tow truck driving has given many drivers special memories. Henry Vanden Heuvel survived a collision in his tow truck. The driver of the car that hit his tow truck died at the accident scene. Henry says he could write a book about his towing career.

Hap Cramer began his towing business not long after he began shaving and he says he would start all over again, more than 40 years later, if he had the chance.

Bill Middleton, Bob Gilder, Jay Lorenz and Tom Ratliff grew up in families that owned towing businesses. Betty Parnham enjoys the business and the trucks so much she's decorated her home in miniature tow trucks.

The unique trucks, the evolution of towing equipment and the dedicated men and women of the towing business all can be found in these pages.

Tow Trucks: A Photographic History has a collection of towing images gathered from many corners of the world. It also is a treasury of towing lore and memories. This book is a tribute to all of those who work the city streets, busy highways and country roads, helping people in need.

We hope you enjoy this book as much as we've enjoyed putting it together. It's for all those who've ever climbed behind the wheel of a tow truck and all those who have wished they could.

John Gunnell and Tom Collins
Dec. 22, 2003

CHAPTER 1
BEGINNINGS

ORIGINS OF THE TOWING INDUSTRY

By John Gunnell

An Aug. 23, 1942 article in Chattanooga Industry magazine claimed the first twin-boom tow truck evolved from a 1916 accident in which a Model T Ford slid into a Tennessee creek. John A. Wiley, the Ford's owner, called Ernest Holmes to retrieve his car. Previously, Holmes had developed some vehicle recovery equipment for his own use in 1915.

Suddenly, he was being called on to test its commercial application.

"After working for a day with the clumsy equipment he was able to amass, he finally brought the vehicle back up the road," said author Fred Hixon.

"That experience made Holmes think. 'Why couldn't some kind of a machine be designed and built which could simplify the handling of wrecked and disabled automobiles?'"

According to Hixon, Holmes was experienced in working with automobiles and trucks. He'd been in the garage business since 1903. Holmes drew up plans for a wrecker on a sheet of paper. A prototype was assembled by

A page from the 1963 **Chevrolet Silver Book** *highlights the long history of the Earnest Holmes Co. by noting its pioneering work in the development of wrecker equipment "for the past 48 years." (OCW)*

local foundries and machine shops in the fall of 1917. Holmes received orders for two tow trucks that same year. Were they the first of their kind? Maybe, or maybe not.

Manley Manufacturing Co. also claimed to have built the first wrecker. An advertisement placed by the company in a 1925 issue of Motor Age magazine stated: "…the auto wrecking crane was originated by Robert E. Manley in 1917."

It stated this was the first auto-wrecking crane to be manufactured and offered to American dealers and garage men. Manley also laid claim to inventing the self-contained saddle, a device that distributes a towed vehicle's weight on the chassis of the tow vehicle, so that its base occupies minimal space.

Whether Earnest Holmes or Robert Manley developed the very first tow truck, it is documented that Holmes soon was selling his machines to auto repair shop and garage owners who were interested in retrieving wrecked or disabled cars.

The first Holmes manufacturing facility was a small shop on Market St. in Chattanooga, Tennessee. His company grew quickly as the automobile industry itself expanded. Eventually, Holmes towing products earned a world-wide reputation for quality and performance.

Other companies—such as Weaver, Taylor-Made, Hubbard and Stringfellow—made early wrecker and tow truck equipment, although none of these brands became

Hubbard Manufacturing Co. of Farmland, Indiana, offered a 10 to 15-ton heavy-duty winch and a semi-crane in the 1963 Chevrolet Silver Book. By that time, Hubbard had been producing wreckers for 40 years. (OCW)

Another Tennessee-based wrecker equipment manufacturer was W. T. Stringfellow and Co., Inc. of Nashville. Four of the firm's 1963 offerings are in this advertisement: the DBS-12, the MW-10, the Mustang light-duty wrecker with a 55L body and the Mustang mounted on a 1950s Chevy pickup. (OCW)

quite as popular as Holmes. The demand for tow trucks grew so strong that Earnest Holmes quit the garage business to make wreckers on a full-time basis. He had to move into a new and larger facility. By 1939, Holmes moved to a location on East 43rd St., in Chattanooga and 69 employees were on the payroll. This number rose to about 200 after World War II broke out. Hundreds of Holmes wreckers were used in battlefield vehicle recoveries.

Ernest Holmes Sr. died on June 10, 1945. Ernest Jr. took over the company at that point. The founder's son, who had served as chief engineer and vice president, now became president. Under his leadership, the product line and the company continued to expand. Holmes was a leader in the towing equipment industry until well after the end of World War II.

Today, the number of manufacturers of wreckers and towing equipment has grown. Miller Industries of Chattanooga is the maker of Century, Holmes, Challenger and Champion wreckers. Other well-known brands include AATAC, Chevron, Danco, Dynamic, Hy-Tech, Jerr-Dan, Kilar, NoMar, Pierce, Trebron, Vulcan, Weld Built and Zacklift.

An advertisement from a 1920s edition of the Automobile Trade Journal depicts a Weaver Auto Crane with a Model T Ford coupe in tow. Other illustrations highlight the features of this device. (OCW)

TOWING WAS TAUGHT AT A KANSAS CITY TRADE SCHOOL

By John Gunnell

Kansas City businessman H.J. Rahe's (pronounced Ray's) Auto and Tractor School operated in the car-repair industry's infant days. Blacksmiths repaired early autos, but by the time the Model T came out in 1908, private vocational schools were training mechanics to fix cars, trucks, tractors and airplanes.

Rahe set up his "big school" with separate departments to teach different systems. Students were taught how to cast and pour engine bearings. They learned how to take apart, assemble and adjust all kinds of carburetors and countless other skills.

No charts or books were used. Everything was done "hands on" using actual vehicle components. The school's well-equipped machine shops featured the latest equipment like power hack saws and South Bend screw cutting lathes.

Repairs weren't the only thing students learned at the school. In addition to hands-on skills, they were taught how to run successful auto-repair businesses.

At that time, in addition to fixing cars, such businesses frequently ran towing services, operated car-storage facilities and included charging stations where batteries could be "juiced up." Many repair shops also sold cars that they purchased after breakdowns or accidents. The damaged cars were towed to the shop and fixed.

Rahe's Auto & Tractor School was set up just like a business. It operated its own tow truck. If a Kansas City motorist had an accident, he or she could call the school and Rahe would purchase the wreck, tow it to the school, and let the students work on it. When the car was repaired, he'd resell it at a tidy profit.

The Dunning Brothers may have been Rahe's graduates. They operated this full-service garage 33 miles from Sacramento, California. In addition to selling genuine Ford parts, they used a cut-down roadster with a wrecker boom as a service car. (John Gunnell)

The unheated Buick garage had a dirt floor and was very cold in winter. Jim Parsons notes: "Service men and tow truck operators had a hard life in the 1920s." (Jim Parsons)

Jim Parson's great uncle owned a garage in Birea, Kentucky, where he sold Crown gasoline and Mohawk tires. They used a cut-down car with a Weaver Auto Crane. (Jim Parsons)

Typically, students attended Rahe's Auto and Tractor School for a period of 1-1/2 to two months. Arthur C. Herrick of Muscatine, Iowa, took six weeks of training. After graduating, he wrote to the school.

"I am happy to report my earnings have tripled since graduation," Herrick wrote. "While I had worked as a mechanic before attending your school, new skills have allowed me to increase my wages by $2.50 a week, but it is due to learning how to operate a towing service and fixing autos for resale that my monthly income has practically doubled in only half a year."

In taking cars and trucks apart and putting them back together, instructors at the school focused on time-saving tips. The school's catalog told the story of a veteran mechanic coming back to learn better ways to do his job. "One day, in the big repair shop, the instructor asked him how he would make a certain repair and how long it would

take. He told the instructor how he would do it and that it would take about three hours. The instructor showed him a way of making this repair that would require only 30 minutes time and the repair would be made much better."

The instructors taught how cutting repair times left more hours of each day for hauling in rebuilders. "A full-service business is necessary to get customers," the teacher said. "But your biggest profits will be realized in selling non-operating cars that you can purchase cheaply, tow to your shop and fix-up for a new owner."

"Men came to Rahe's from every state in the Union and from foreign countries," H. J. Rahe claimed.

His Auto & Tractor School helped many of them to become successful independent auto servicemen. "Hundreds of Rahe graduates are in business for themselves," boasted the proud educator back in 1917.

Jim Parsons of Lexington, Kentucky, sent this photo of his grandfather and other men he worked with at a Buick garage in Harlan, Kentucky. (Jim Parsons)

CUT-UP CLASSICS MADE REGAL WRECKERS

By John Gunnell

The classic cars of today — Packards, Lincolns and Pierce-Arrows — had very little value as used cars during the Depression and were worth practically nothing just after World War II. Poor fuel mileage hurt their early used-car values. And by the late '40s, they seemed archaic. Even scrap yards didn't really want them, except for the few that wore custom aluminum bodies — and then only because the value of aluminum was high.

A decent classic worthy of taking to a car show today could be bought off the back row of a used-car lot for $50 in the late-'30s, while an economical used Ford, Chevy or Plymouth would bring more.

Some buyers had a use for the "big iron" — garage and gas station owners who operated wrecker services.

In those days, many of these independent garage men couldn't afford a factory-built, truck-based tow truck. However, they were handy enough to cut down the body of a classic passenger car, then mount a wrecker hoist in the rumble seat or rear passenger compartment. The result was a rig that was as sturdy as any brand-new 1-ton truck and usually half again as powerful. Almost all such cars had at least an eight-cylinder engine and many were V-12 or even V-16-powered.

Like the tow vehicles, many of the hoists mounted on them were take-offs from older tow trucks or possibly home-fabricated. It didn't make much sense to these frugal grease monkeys to pay $250 or $300 for a 1- or 1-1/2-ton crane from Weaver, Little Giant or Manley to install on a $50 truck. Naturally, an expensive, cable-rigged Holmes model

Bryan Betz was 22-years-old in 1930 when he operated the Standard Garage on Highway 66 in Sullivan, Missouri. His wrecker was a converted touring car. (Charles J. Betz)

A 1924 Lincoln had a second life as a tow car for Johnson's Garage of Minier, Illinois. Lincolns, Cadillacs, Packards and other large cars often were converted for towing. (John Gunnell)

with adjustable booms was entirely out of the question.

Usually, the parts for the hoist came from the scrap pile "out back" of the garage in those pre-EPA-era days. Some old automobile frame rails bolted together in A-frame style and fitted with pulleys, chains and a crank arm would do fine. In many instances, an old "torpedo" style headlamp from a pre-war car would be mounted near the crane to illuminate night-time rescue operations.

According to some old timers, the frames from the Essex (a small Hudson-built model) were best suited for homemade hoists, since their rear spring hangers had a unique offset that eased construction. A pin through the holes drilled in the frame for mounting spring shackles provided a handy place to mount a pulley or sheave at the tip of the boom.

Other garages simply mounted "speed hoists" — the type used to yank engines and commonly seen hanging from the ceiling of old repair shops. The speed hoists were temporarily suspended from a hook on a boom attached to the back of an older classic car. When the towing work was over, the speed hoist could be unhooked from the wrecking boom and re-attached to the shop's ceiling to do double duty.

The great truck historian Rolland Jerry, of Canada, reported seeing such a setup on a 1927 Studebaker Big Six used by a Depression-era shop called the Square Deal Garage. But, as Jerry noted, Cadillacs seemed to be the brand of car most often chosen for wrecker conversions. Classic Caddys had a rugged three-spring rear platform suspension, beefy rear frame cross members and powerful V-8, V-12 or V-16 engines.

When working with a sedan body, the converters often made a closed-cab wrecker by neatly removing the entire rear portion of the body with the rear window and curved upper body corners intact.

Next, they removed doors and panels behind the front seat, leaving the center body pillars. They moved the rear portion of the body forward and attached it behind the center pillar. A bit of welding resulted in a closed truck cab with a built-in rear window. In most cases, the body width was similar enough at all points to allow a neat, clean grafting. The final step was mounting the hoist where the sedan's rear seat had been.

In the case of a coupe or convertible, much cutting and welding was eliminated. Instead, the deck lid and rumble seat (if so equipped) were removed and the hoist was mounted below the area where the deck lid had been. Of course, there were many variations on these themes. Leaving the rear side panels of the sedan's body in place formed a pickup-style cargo box around the hoist. This area provided storage space for tools and equipment.

Some mechanics got so good at converting classic cars into wreckers they made conversion a regular sideline. Around 1940, at least one garage owner specialized in modifying Packards this way for a set price of about $1,000. Estimating $50 for the classic car, $250 for the hoist and another $100 for supplies, that was still a $600 profit, which went a long way in the early '40s.

Naturally, the market for car-into-wrecker conversions declined rapidly after World War II. By that time, automobiles with 1/4-inch thick, eight-inch deep frame rails had passed into automotive history. In addition, the economy was booming, and buying a shiny new, purpose-built tow truck seemed to make good sense.

O'Hare Truck Service brought this tow car conversion to the 1991 Iola Old Car Show. It was made from a 1929 Chrysler Model 65 coupe. (Ron Kowalke)

HOOKED ON YOU

By John Gunnell

Some years ago, the International Towing and Recovery Museum, in Chattanooga, Tenn., announced it had received a donation of antique vehicle-towing tools from Dixie Industries. Getting this gift was a nice addition to the museum's regular collection of restored vintage tow trucks.

The towing tools and equipment, which appeared to be strange-looking to the general public, really gave museum visitors the idea that it takes more than a truck and a boom to "hook" onto a vehicle when it's damaged or illegally parked.

Dixie Industries is a Chattanooga-based company and a division of Columbus McKinnon Corp. The company's parent firm traces its roots and its tool and equipment making history back to 1875. That was the year that L. E. McKinnon first began making hardware for horse-drawn carriages. Just after the dawn of the automobile age, it evolved into the towing equipment business.

From these humble beginnings, Columbus McKinnon Corp. has grown into North America's largest manufacturer of hoists, operator-controlled manipulators and alloy chain. The company designs, produces and sells (mainly to distributors) a wide-ranging line of material handling, lifting and positioning devices for domestic and international markets. The vehicle-recovery industry is one of its biggest markets.

The tools were proudly displayed at the Chattanooga museum and included a complete collection of J-hooks, belts, and other types of hooks and chains. A display of belts and chains used by vehicle-recovery professionals also were part of the exhibit. The collection even traced the steps involved in making eye-slip hooks for vehicle recovery work. Other elements of the collection included books on the history of the local company and some of its product manuals from the old days.

Dixie Industries' gift made it possible for the International Towing and Recovery Museum to better educate the general public about some fascinating devices

A joy bar, towing sling, chains and J-hooks attached to a postwar Willys Jeep pickup are ready to tow in this close-up photo. (John Gunnell)

This display at the International Towing and Recovery Museum in Chattanooga, Tennessee, traced steps in making eye-slip hooks for vehicle recovery work. (Dixie Industries)

Weld-Built Body Co., Brooklyn, New York, offered a variety of towing accessories in this 1962 advertisement. (OCW)

used in the towing industry.

Those who never have operated a wrecker or worked for a towing service can go through life without ever seeing a forged-web sling-end attachment, a two-legged bridle-chain assembly or other vehicle recovery hardware. The museum's display gives the average viewer some extra insight about the tower's role in American history.

For information about the International Towing and Recovery Museum call (423) 267-3132.

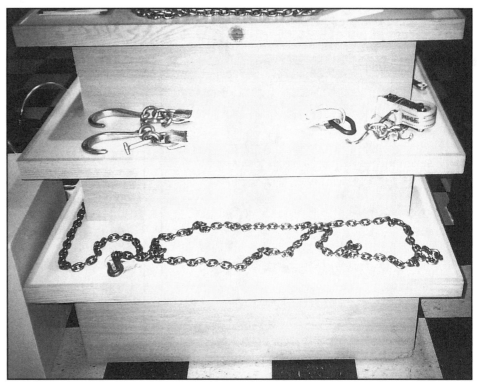

A display of belts and chains used by vehicle-recovery professionals was a part of the International Towing and Recovery Museum exhibit. (Dixie Industries)

A LIFTING EXPERIENCE By John Gunnell

The average person hearing the name "Holmes" would probably think of a famous, fictitious Scotland Yard detective. The average vehicle-recovery professional would think of the great tow truck bodies made by Ernest Holmes Co., of Chattanooga. Few people today, even towing professionals, would think about the repair shop equipment the Tennessee wrecker manufacturing company made many years ago.

When you think about it, Ernest Holmes Co.'s involvement in supplying garage men with items such as automobile lifting devices was entirely logical. In the first place, a tow truck itself is a lifting device on wheels. In the second place, many of the pioneering tow men who operated in the industry's early days also did auto repairs.

The Holmes Universal Auto-Lift of the early 1930s was designed for speeding up automotive repairs, lubrication, washing, polishing and general servicing. The device raised and lowered cars by supporting and lifting their front and rear axles. When the car was in the air, the steering gear, wheels and wheel assemblies were free for greasing, repairs and adjustments.

An electrically-driven screw used a series of gears to force the steel links out of the base. A steel shaft passed through each link, forcing it to assume a vertical position. The links then automatically interlocked, creating four tremendously strong upright columns that supported the car up in the air.

When the steel links were collapsed in the base, the Holmes Universal Auto-Lift was only seven inches high, but when they were formed into the support columns, the lift was raised to 4 ft. 8 in. high. It was 5 ft. 4 in. wide, 21 ft. 10 in. long, weighed 2,100 lbs. and had a 6,000-lb. lifting capacity. It was the only automotive lifting device approved by Universal Laboratories in its day.

Two big advantages of the Holmes lift were it didn't have to be buried or bolted down. For mechanics who rented their shop, that was good news. If they later moved to a bigger facility, they could take their Holmes Auto-Lift with them. The manufacturer said that it could be loaded on a truck in 30 minutes and could be operating again, in a new location, in "approximately the same time."

At that time, in the '30s, many mechanics used pits dug into the ground as a way to gain access to the underside of automobiles. Such pits could be a great danger, as gasoline fumes would collect in them and could cause explosions. An above-ground lift eliminated this extremely dangerous type of situation. The Holmes Universal Auto-Lift also required no concrete work, no plumbing, no air connections and no assembly or installation costs.

The lift came largely put together. The purchaser of the device simply had to attach a set of guide rails between the two column. These were attached to the lift by a simple clamping device. When installed, they helped to center the vehicle being lifted. The lifts extended out to the sides, to fit the track of the car. The electric motor supplied with the lift came completely pre-wired and with a safety control switch. The electric motor was a 3-phase, 60-cycle unit that developed two horsepower. Both 220-volt and 440-volt motors were available.

Back in the days when Holmes was marketing the Universal Auto-Lift, the company used the advertising slogan "It Takes a Holmes to Do It" to promote its full line of products. Tow truck operators who used Holmes wreckers to deal with emergencies at all hours of the day knew that there was a lot of truth behind that motto. And those who also worked on the cars that they towed, often turned to Holmes when it came to equipping their shops with lifting devices and other heavy-duty hardware.

A mechanic works on the back end of a 1920s closed sedan raised aloft by the Holmes Lift. (Bob Pierce)

CHAPTER 2
TRUCK MAKERS

DODGE
CHRYSLER
Dodge Trucks
De Soto
IMPERIAL
PLYMOUTH

DAY AND NIGHT SERVICE

PHONE
880

Dearth

WLAD 880

BRAND LOYAL NEW-CAR DEALERS' "BRAND-LOYAL" WRECKERS

By John Gunnell

Most modern towing services are operated in a professional, business-like manner. This wasn't always true in the "good old days" when countless small shops ran wreckers on a free-lance basis. Such operations were often reluctant offshoots of a repair shop and homemade equipment (such as converted passenger cars with booms) was the rule.

The shiny wreckers operated by dealers who sold new cars and trucks often had a few distinctive characteristics. They were newer and cleaner than their counterparts operated by private garages or used-car dealers. They often advertised the brand of vehicles the dealer sold, rather than the towing service itself. Many trucks wore the same nameplate that was on the new cars in the dealer's showroom.

In old photos from the 1920s and 1930s, Ford, Studebaker and Hudson stand out as the automakers that had the strongest programs to induce their dealers to use tow trucks as promotional tools. Whether the automakers required dealers to show brand loyalty or it was a sense of pride is a fact that didn't turn up in research. One might surmise it was a combination of both, plus simple economics, that explains the trucks seen in such photos.

Economics and image also explain why dealer trucks often were newer and cleaner than those run by private towing services. Franchised dealers typically were wealthy enough to afford the latest tow truck model. Most did sufficient business each year to justify annual replacement of their recovery vehicles. There may have also been factory discounts for dealers who used trucks of the same brands that they sold.

In 1941, a man named Ebersole operated dealerships with Oldsmobile and Pontiac franchises in two Pennsylvania towns, Cleona and Lebanon. Although Oldsmobile had produced some large trucks in the teens and Pontiac had made a Deluxe Delivery for two years in the mid-'20s, neither automaker was building trucks in the World War II era. Mr. Ebersole did the next logical thing and used a 1941 GMC wrecker at his dealership. In October 1999, the restored truck was brought to the Antique Automobile Club of America's giant car show in Hershey, Pa. This pretty towing machine pulled in many Olds and Pontiac owners — and not always on a hook.

Diamond T Motor Car Co. of Chicago, Ill, made some of the prettiest tow trucks around right after World War II. Sturdy and pricey, they easily caught the eye of anyone who saw them in action.

As we mentioned above, some dealers sold brands that didn't offer trucks. The Buick, Olds or Pontiac dealer could turn to GMC, the Lincoln-Mercury dealer could run a Ford tow truck and a Chrysler or Plymouth dealer could use a truck by Dodge.

This 1941 GMC tow truck is a proud symbol of Ebersole Inc., a Pontiac, Buick and GMC dealership in Cleona and Lebanon, Pennsylvania. (Ron Kowalke)

CHEVROLET
CHEVROLET LISTED TOWING EQUIPMENT IN "SILVER BOOKS"

By John Gunnell

First published in the 1930s, the Silver Book is a catalog of "engineered vocational equipment" for Chevrolet trucks produced annually by Verbiest Publishing Co. of Michigan. The companies listed in the Silver Books made bodies and equipment for all variations of Chevrolet commercial vehicles. Each company was a select vendor that Chevrolet Motor Division "approved" to supply such things as garbage-truck and school-bus bodies or winches and snow plows.

Silver Books listed the specifications for the different types of Chevy trucks ranging from El Caminos all the way up to the big Medium-Duty rigs. (That included the over-the-road Bison, Bruin and Titan highway semi-tractors made in the years 1970-1980.) This section included wheelbases, weights, chassis lengths and widths, weights, tire sizes, cab dimensions, seating configurations, and more.

Another section consisted of full-page advertisements from various body and equipment suppliers organized by the types of bodies or equipment they sold. For example, there would be 10 ads from companies that made delivery-van bodies, then the next five pages would show fire-truck bodies made by different firms. Some companies produced a variety of products and they would usually have just one ad with a list of their market niches.

The 1962 Chevrolet Silver Book included seven pages of ads from wrecker makers. Canfield Tow Bar Company

WORLD'S MOST WIDELY USED WRECKER

HOLMES ENGINEERING HAS NO EQUAL in the WRECKER FIELD!

47 YEARS of PIONEERING in WRECKER DEVELOPMENT

HOLMES is the world's most widely used WRECKER simply because, *HOLMES Engineering has NO equal in wrecker performance.* The standard of working efficiency provided in the new HOLMES models is an engineering accomplishment that has taken more than 47 years to achieve. The power-operated, double boom type wrecker originated by HOLMES, although *never* basically changed, has been continually improved. Over the years many new and exclusive features have been added to obtain greater flexibility, load capacity and operating efficiency. It is these factors which have established *HOLMES Superiority . . . and World-Wide Acceptance.* Today, only HOLMES offers such a background of manufacturing experience and engineering progress in wrecker development. Send for full details, including name of your local distributor.

THIS → **IDENTIFIES Your Local DISTRIBUTOR**

HOLMES Wreckers **AUTHORIZED SALES**

HOLMES offers WIDE Choice of Models for CHEVROLET TRUC

330-H MODEL — 3 TON WRECKER. Hand operated. Built small for light work. Handles all cars and many other jobs around every shop. For CHEVROLET models C & K14 through C-40. Minimum GVW 4,800 lbs.

400 MODEL—4 TON WRECKER Small yet sturdy. Built for light pick-up and towing. Handles all cars and numerous types of service calls. For CHEVROLET models C & K25 through C-40. Minimum GVW 5,800 lbs.

460 MODEL — 6 TON WRECKER For light pick-up and towing of all cars. Fast, flexible, easy to maneuver in city traffic. Rated capacity 3 tons per boom. For CHEVROLET models C-36 through C-40. Min., GVW 7,000 lbs.

470 MODEL—8 TON WRECKER Handles all cars and light trucks. Fast, versatile, well suited for work in congested areas and on winding ramps. Rated capacity 4 tons per boom. For CHEVROLET models C-36 through C, L & T 60. Min., GVW 9,500 lbs.

525 MODEL—12 TON WRECKER All p unit. Handles all cars and average Has long range of operation, cap wide variety of work. Rated capacity per boom. For CHEVROLET model through C, L & T 60. Min., GVW 13,5

650 MODEL— 20 TON WRECKER B Heavy Duty work yet fast and enough to be economically used on li and trucks. Rated capacity 10 tons per For CHEVROLET models C & L-60-H t C, L & M-80. Min., GVW 22,000 lbs.

850 MODEL—40 TON WRECKER Built for handling all large trucks, buses, trailers, etc., too big and heavy for the average wrec Rated capacity 20 tons per boom. Recommended for use on CHEVROLET model M-78 Tandem. Minimum GVW 30,000 lbs.

ERNEST HOLMES COMPANY . . . CHATTANOOGA 7, TENN., U.S.

The 1962 Silver Book Holmes ad said it made the "World's Most Widely Used Wreckers." (OCW)

had its ad on page 65. The Douglas Motors Corp. ad was on page 62. Ernest Holmes had an ad on page 63. Hubbard's ad was on page 64. Weld-Built Body Co. took page 67 and Western's Wrecker Division advertised on page 62.

The Marysville Body Works had its ad on page 134. The latter ad showed only utility and fire-truck bodies, but

Chevrolet factory-approved wrecker bodies, like the one on this 1978 K30 truck chassis, were ordered through the Silver Book. (OCW)

the Boyertown, Pennsylvania, company would build you a wrecker if you really wanted one and had the money to pay for it.

The index sections of a typical Silver Book were listings of advertisers sorted by the categories they fit into. One index might include "Equipment and Accessory" suppliers and include categories for Towing Equipment, Towing Hoists and Towing Hooks. The "Truck Body" index usually listed companies that built "Wrecker" bodies. The third index—for "Trailers and Trailer Bodies" – sometimes had wrecker or towing listings.

Silver Books were strictly for Chevrolet buyers. They were distributed on the basis of one catalog to every Chevy dealer in the nation. Other truck makers had similar catalogs. Hildy's Ford Blue Book was for Ford truck buyers. GMC called its catalog the Vocational Equipment Directory. The Star Directory was International's counterpart. No doubt, Dodge had its own catalog, too.

Tow-truck history buffs or restorers will want to look for catalogs of this type at flea markets or on e-Bay. If you find one, you'll enjoy reading the advertisements and seeing the tow-truck bodies and equipment that were available years ago.

CHALLENGER E-920H Series

R/700 Series

E-80 ELECTRA Series

For heavy-duty work it's AW CHALLENGER E-920H. Handles all towing, recovery and light crane work. Boom capacity 22 tons — 6- to 8-foot boom extension takes loads up to 7 tons at 45 degrees — dual rear controls — body jacks — gas throttle — 2 speeds forward and speed reverse PTO. A big rig to handle big jobs and make big profits.

R-700 Series AW Wreckers are individually engineered for light, medium, or heavy work. Each vehicle is designed to handle a specific maximum tonnage. The range is between 4 to 12 tons. Boom extensions are up to 6 feet with maximum load of 6 tons. Dual rear controls - 2-way PTO. R-700's have AW's famous, exclusive 360 degrees ROTOHEAD. Permits full circle winching or retrieving uphill, downhill, horizontal. The wrecker that puts money in your pocket.

For light jobs up to 4 tons — it's the low cost money-maker — E-80 ELECTRA. Operates on vehicle's 12-volt battery — finger-tip controls — weather protected circuits — optional boom extension. Self-locking worm and gear safety. Rig fits 1/2-, 3/4-, 1-ton pick-ups. Economical in operation, high in profits.

All AW bodies have modern, low silhouette styling — heavy welded construction — double-flanged tailplate with towing rings — heavy-duty floor sills — recessed tail lights — contoured wheel openings — cargo space — body steps (larger models) — tool compartments (some models) — bodies and rigs transferable.

Whatever the Challenge... One of these Powerful AW Wreckers can Handle it!

WRITE OR PHONE TODAY FOR YOUR DEMONSTRATION.

AW

AMERICAN WRECKERS INC.

23375 Dequindre Road
Hazel Park, Michigan 48030
phone (313) 544-0150

(Formerly A & W Tow Truck Mfg. Co.)
Distributorships Available

American Wrecker, Hazel Park, Michigan, offered its Challenger E-920H, R/700 and E-80 Electra series for trucks in the 1969 Silver Book. (OCW)

This 1962 Chevrolet 60 carries an approved wrecker body that would have been advertised in that year's edition of the **Silver Book.** *(OCW)*

Canfield Tow Bar Company used the **Silver Book** *to promote its wrecker equipment for light and medium-duty Chevy trucks. (OCW)*

A 1972 Chevrolet C60 with a 427 V-8 belonged to Henry's Incorporated of Kaukauna, Wisconsin. (Henry Vanden Heuvel)

A 1929 Chevrolet International model with Weaver tow crane originally belonged to Shinner Brothers Garage, Atlanta, Missouri. It has just over 17,000 original miles. (Richard Sorrels)

Hap Cramer's 1961 Chevrolet Viking 60 tow truck included bucket seats from an Impala Super Sport and was powered by a Corvette V-8. (Hap Cramer)

A 1950s-era Chevrolet tow truck prepares to pull a 1959 Chevrolet Impala two-door hardtop out of trouble. (Brian Furman)

CANYONVILLE'S HOME-GROWN CHEVY TOW TRUCK

By Tom Collins

Some people just come to mind when you think of a hometown. Their entire life has revolved around a community they've known since birth. People recognize them and over the years, they've experienced a lot of joys and sorrows in the community. They're deeply rooted in one place.

Canyonville, Oregon, population 1,219, according to the 1990 U.S. Census, is a hometown to be proud of. Located along Interstate 5, it's near Crater Lake, Canyon Mountain and the Umpqua Forest and Wilderness Area. Popular attractions include camping, fishing and swimming,

as well as the Seven Feathers Casino and Resort.

One venerable citizen of Canyonville is a 1950 Chevrolet COE with a 525 Holmes wrecker attached, now owned by Bill's Towing of that city. It's used in area parades and occasionally goes to shows but its family history makes the truck even more interesting.

"It was the first 'store bought' wrecker in Canyonville," says Leon Oaks, second generation owner of Oaks Garage. "Before this Chevy, all of the others were used trucks."

The original owner brought the spanking new 1950 Chevrolet 5400 series COE home to Canyonville more

The Oaks Garage in Canyonville, Oregon, was the third owner of the 1950 Chevrolet tow truck. Before it became a show truck, it was a hard working Canyonville citizen. (Bill Oaks)

The Canyonville Chevy helps a stranded motorist after an Oregon snowstorm. (Bill Oaks)

than 53 years ago. It was used at a truck stop for a few years—a location now covered by a Highway 5 overpass. In the early '50s, the Chevy found a new home, at a Canyonville body shop owned by a man named Jack Swearington.

In 1956, Ed Oaks, Leon's dad, bought the Chevy for his Oaks Garage. At the time, it was painted green, gold and cream. Ed and his young son, Leon, changed the color and soon made some internal improvements to the Chevy.

The Chevrolet's original "low pressure" 235 6-cylinder engine was replaced with a more powerful version made in the mid '50s. Later, a 283 cid V-8 was the engine of choice. For several years, it ran with a 327 cid Chevy truck V-8.

Through the years, the 5-speed transmission has been rock solid. One of Ed Oaks' additions in the late '50s was a Timken two-speed rear axle. The veteran Chevrolet always has sported a 525 Holmes towing unit.

The bulk of its life was spent with the Oaks Garage where the durable Chevy was a good match with Ed, who worked until he was 81. He decided to wind down his work to care for his ailing spouse.

"It was the only wrecker dad and I had," says Leon. "We used it for everything. We pulled a cow from a well and even a horse from a septic tank. Sometimes the front end would go up a bit. And the springs strained under some heavy loads."

"Originally, we painted it white with red booms, then later painted the booms black. We made no other modifications other than making some slings dad made from some pipes and belting—before that sort of thing was sold on the market."

Like a good friend, the Chevy always was ready to provide reliable service through the years. In 1996, Bill's Tires, Towing and Automotive bought it for secondary uses in parades and other attractions. By that time, technology finally had overcome the Chevy's durability as wheel lifts and a new generation of equipment took over the towing industry.

Today, the Chevy is a show stopper painted in two shades of metallic colors and wearing chromed wheels, front bumper and grille as well as other trim work.

Current owner, Bill Nicholson, has respected the Chevy's enduring past with a cartoon of it in action on its side quarter panels as well as a credit to the Oaks Garage on the truck.

An honored citizen throughout its life, today the hard-working Chevrolet has become a Canyonville icon. One very solid citizen.

DIAMOND T HISTORICAL PHOTO OF STREAMLINED 1935 DIAMOND T TELLS A STORY

By John Gunnell

Every photo of old cars and trucks tells a story. Armed with a magnifying glass and couple of research books, you may be lucky enough to turn an image that someone snapped 50, 60 or 70 years ago into a piece of history. And if you're lucky, you may even find several different pieces of history that fit together and heighten the details of your historic research.

The accompanying photo of a handsome-looking Diamond T tow truck is a good example. Diamond T Motor Car Company built some of the prettiest wreckers and other types of trucks that ever left an assembly line. A book that the Chicago-based company published in 1952 showed pictures of many of its dealerships in different regions of the country.

"Some of these dealers' establishments are as large and as attractive as passenger car showrooms," said the book's introduction. "Others are quite the opposite—extremely modest and business-like in appearance. But they all have one thing in common—they provide the finest, most efficient service it is possible to offer at the lowest possible cost."

Whether that boast was true, the book was filled with many charming black and white photos of the exteriors and interiors of Diamond T dealerships across the country.

Some of these franchises also operated wrecker services. In some pictures, you can see tow trucks parked inside or outside the dealership buildings.

A paper pocket glued to the book's inside rear cover contained a complete directory of all the Diamond T agencies from coast to coast. The 11-page directory had

A gorgeous 1935 Diamond T 1 to 1-1/2 ton wrecker. The body was made by National Steel Products Co. of Kansas City. (Joe Egle)

about 50 listings per page. Some simple math will show you there were 550 dealers.

The Diamond T truck seen in the old photo is a real "looker." It has a stylish "fat-fendered" front end, a rather high hood line and a straight-back cowl molding. At the rear is a high-side service truck body complete with bright metal trim rails. The body features built-in cabinets and built-in taillights. The rear fenders are dressed up with some art deco-style fender skirts.

The Diamond T was outfitted with a single, adjustable towing boom—at least a four tonner. At the rear of the truck was a hitch setup and a tow joy. The tire for a wheel dolly laid on the truck's bed, below the boom. Printle hooks and even a spotlight were mounted at the lower rear section of the body.

The hood nameplate and louver treatment seen on the truck are consistent with the 1935 Diamond T—probably a "200" Series model in the 1-1/2 to 2-ton category. Seeing how pretty this particular truck is, it's hard to believe the chassis price was only $575 when it was new. The completed tow truck, with all the wrecker equipment, probably sold for less than $1,500.

The truck's door carried the logo of M & E Auto Body Works. Lettering on the back of the cab and sides indicates M & E was located at the intersection of 4th St. and State Ave. in Kansas City, Kansas. Other lettering says "We Fix Wrecks" and "24 Hour Service" and gives the phone number as "Drexel 3134."

Flipping through the 1952 directory of Diamond T dealers reveals the company had only seven factory dealers in Kansas at that time. They were located in the towns of Goodland, Lawrence, Mineola, Salina, Topeka, Wamego and Wichita, but not Kansas City.

Diamond T's often were quite fancy rigs with chrome grilles, chrome hood ornaments, cab and fender clearance lights, chrome door lettering and chrome hubcaps. (Applegate and Applegate)

There was a dealer called Diamond T Truck Sales at 2605 Warwick Trafficway in Kansas City, Missouri. There's a good chance this agency may have sold the handsome tow truck in 1935.

Also consider the impact of World War II. American involvement started just six years after the 1935 Diamond T tow truck was new and delayed many changes the country would have gone through from 1941 to 1946 under normal conditions. There is a very good chance Diamond T Truck Sales of Kansas City, Missouri, looked much the same in the early '50s as it had in 1935. It could have handled the original sale of this truck. What do you think?

A 1951 Diamond T Model 420, owned by the District of Columbia's Metropolitan Police Department, keeps a no parking zone clear in front of the Capitol building. (Applegate and Applegate)

GREEN DIAMOND LOGO STOOD FOR QUALITY

By John Gunnell

Although the company built great trucks and top-notch wreckers, Diamond T Motor Car Co. actually started off as an automaker in 1905. Six years later, a customer asked owner C.A. Tilt to make a truck and the die was cast for a long history of truck making.

From 1911 through 1958, the firm operated as the Diamond T Motor Car Co. of Chicago, Illinois. Then it became the Diamond T Motor Truck Co., also based in Chicago. The Diamond T Division of White Motor Co. was its name from 1961-1966, when it moved to Lansing, Michigan. It then became the Diamond Reo Truck Division of White Motor Corp., until 1971. Diamond Reo Trucks, Inc., lasted until 1975. Osterlund, Inc., of Harrisburg, Pennsylvania, took over in 1977 and produced a limited number of Diamond Reo trucks.

Diamond Reo became associated with a trucks parts and equipment company based in Harrisburg that ultimately purchased the assets and inventory of Osterlund in December 1995. The two companies had a complex, intertwined relationship and became involved in a 2001 lawsuit related to truck cabs built for the Oregon firm Mid Pacific Industries. Though settled in favor of Diamond Reo Truck Corporation, little is known about the company beyond that point.

The first Diamond T truck, built in 1911, was a conventional four-cylinder vehicle that was used in Chicago until as late as 1930. Identifying this truck was a green diamond logo with a "T" in the middle. The diamond stood for quality and the "T" stood for Tilt.

Diamond T played a major role in the World War I effort by building about 1,500 Liberty trucks in 18 months to support the war effort. This led to more government orders in the postwar period. Diamond T was off and running with a line of 1-1/2- to 5-ton trucks designed for every purpose.

As the tow truck industry started in the 1920s, Diamond T was using six-cylinder engines with four-speed transmissions and spiral-bevel axles. It was making models up to 12-tons.

Combined with great engineering and a well-organized dealer network, Diamond T counted on exceptional styling to increase sales by 60 percent between 1927 and 1928. A fleet of streamlined oil tankers with Heil bodies gained notoriety in the early 1930s.

The 1933 to 1935 period brought the all-steel cab, slanting V windshields and heavily-skirted fenders. Diamond T always seemed to use more chrome than other truck makers. According to company legend, C.A. Tilt was

In 1941, Holmes used this Diamond T COE to showcase its "modernized wrecking and towing equipment." (Applegate and Applegate)

personally responsible for all Diamond T designs.

By 1936, Diamond T trucks were available with diesel engines. That year, sales hit a record 8,750 units. Cab-over-engine models were brought to market in 1937, and proved to be an immediate hit with tow truck operators wanting a shorter wheelbase for better maneuverability. An even bigger sales attraction was the one-year/100,000-mile warranty introduced in 1940.

In 1941, the Ernest Holmes Co. used a Diamond T COE truck to showcase its "modernized wrecking and towing equipment." Holmes' Demonstrator No. 60 carried the company's latest power-operated twin-boom wrecker equipment in a streamlined body with lots of bright metal trim. The heavy-duty Holmes Wrecker unit featured the best in industry technology available at that time.

"Its actual earning ability is amazing and almost unbelievable," said a promotional postcard. "Greater still is its value as an advertising medium. The entire community knows you are progressive — wide awake and a leader in your line."

No Diamond T truck history would be complete without mentioning the company's World War II production and the heavy-duty Diamond T wreckers used on the battlefields of Europe and Asia. When the fighting ended, many military surplus units were purchased by towers all over the country. They were perfect for hauling cars that broke down on the new Interstate Highway System championed by President Eisenhower.

C. A. Tilt retired from his 41-year career at Diamond T in 1946. He continued to serve as chairman of the board until he died in 1956. Early in the postwar period, the company produced 14 models from 2- to 18-tons. Product sales zoomed over the 10,000 mark in 1947 and 1948 and deliveries to towers followed suit. The military tow truck reputation spurred civilian model sales.

Diamond T won design awards in the early '50s and made few major product changes, yet its sales slowly dwindled to the 5,000 to 6,000 range. Partners were needed to keep the business going.

In 1958, White Motor Co. purchased Diamond T and joined Reo, which it already owned. In 1960, operations were moved to Lansing, Michigan. The two brands were marketed separately until 1967, when they were consolidated. New models, introduced on May 1, 1967, were called Diamond Reos.

Francis L. Cappaert, of Birmingham, Alabama, purchased Diamond Reo in 1971 and enacted numerous changes. The firm kept assembly lines rolling and even increased production, but found itself fighting an uphill battle with its aging facilities, financial obligations and fewer government contracts.

The result was bankruptcy in 1975. Consolidated International, an Ohio parts distributor, wound up with the inventory and sold sub-assemblies and parts until Osterlund, Inc. took over in 1977 and built a limited number of Diamond Reos.

For most tow truck buffs, the great Diamond T wreckers of the 1940s and 1950s characterize the company's vast contributions to tow truck history.

This veteran Holmes-equipped 1940s era Diamond T was used by the Denver Fire Department for towing. (Mark Redman)

GREEN DIAMOND LOGO STOOD FOR QUALITY

DODGE
A BRIEF HISTORY
OF DODGE WRECKERS
By John Gunnell

The Dodge car debuted Nov. 14, 1914. The next day the first Dodge "commercial chassis" was made when a Brooklyn, New York, Dodge dealer put a utility body on a car. He wasn't the only one who wanted to see the Dodge Brothers make trucks. In fact it wasn't a single person—it was an army.

In 1916, Gen. John Pershing took a fleet of rugged Dodge automobiles and other vehicles to Mexico to chase the villain Pancho Villa. Pershing thought the Dodges, in particular, performed well and ordered his staff to drive them. The first real Dodge truck was made for the U.S. Army in 1917.

The Army Dodge had stiff truck springs, a steeply-inclined steering wheel and an under-the-seat gas tank. It was available with screen-side or panel bodies.

In a case of "brotherly love," Dodge Brothers signed a 1921 agreement with Graham Brothers to supply parts for Graham trucks, marketing them through Dodge dealers. In 1923, a different series of Dodge trucks was released using passenger car front ends. The next year, Dodge went back to "all-trucks" with longer wheelbases. The last Dodge/Graham trucks, from 1925 and '26, had enclosed cabs with roll-up windows.

In 1925, Chrysler Corporation replaced the Maxwell Corporation, during the time period when Dodge was trying to make its Graham partnership work. On June 1, 1928, Walter P. Chrysler bought Dodge and immediately began using the Dodge Brothers name on all Dodge products, including the trucks.

Dodge Brothers trucks could be ordered with the new Plymouth four-cylinder engine or a Dodge six-cylinder. The Dodge six powered many wreckers as did both straight eight and V-8 Dodge engines produced in later years.

Jim Sutter's pretty 1936 Dodge wrecker showed up at the Antique Automobile Club of America's fall meet in Hershey, Pennsylvania. (John Gunnell)

The 1961 Dodge sales brochure promoted the non-military Power-Wagon four-wheel-drive models as "the trucks that take on tough jobs." (OCW)

Extra care in engineering helped give the 1974 Power-Wagon Sweptline tow trucks their rugged Dodge dependability. (Dodge News)

Redesigned Dodge trucks appeared in 1933 and another redesign in 1936 closely linked the trucks and cars. A ladder-type frame was introduced and added to the sturdiness of Dodges—which became real "trucks" rather than "commercial cars."

The first of many factory-built Dodge 3/4 –ton trucks was assembled in 1937. The 3/4-ton chassis made a good base for small wreckers. Dodge styling was revamped again in 1939, the last year of wood (oak) load compartment floors. Dodge was on the cutting edge of making all-steel wreckers popular.

Sealed-beam headlamps appeared in 1940 Dodges and elsewhere. After minor alterations in 1941 and '42, Dodge went off to war and produced a powerful all-wheel-drive military model that became famous as the civilian Power Wagon.

This heavy-duty 1-ton was the "Hummer" of its day. It offered buyers a power plant on wheels capable of a wide range of industrial, agricultural and towing jobs. The Power Wagon helped make 1946 and '47 record truck-sales years that wouldn't be beat until 1968.

Immediately after World War II, there was a severe shortage of cars and trucks. Auto and truck factories couldn't resume peacetime manufacturing soon enough. Record car output increased the demand for tow trucks as many fine old pre-war wreckers had worn out from extended use during the war years. When people couldn't get new models they kept older models running. As tow calls increased, the older equipment strained under the higher demand.

One unusual Dodge wrecker of this era was a 1949 COE. It was used to load a '53 Dodge convertible from the Jimmy Lynch "Death Dodgers" auto-thrill show onto a '53 Dodge tractor and trailer that carried around the stunt cars.

Dodge trucks got Fluid Drive in 1950. This step toward an automatic transmission required a clutch pedal to shift into primary gears like reverse or low. The fluid coupling shifted the transmission as the driver let up on the accelerator. Large trucks with three-speed manual gearboxes (like wreckers) got a column gearshift. Fully automatic

Stan's Service relied on this 1964 Dodge D500 heavy-duty service truck to handle its towing chores. It had a 15,000 lb., two-speed rear axle and dual rear wheels. (Dodge News)

transmission wasn't used much in tow trucks until it was perfected.

Stylists made revisions to the Dodge grille in 1951 and '52 but made few technical changes. A clean and functional 1951 wrecker was based on a B-3-D 126-in. wheelbase Dodge. While an all-new model was introduced in 1954, the Power Wagon was the Dodge that appealed to most tow truck operators. Rugged and battle-tested, it seemed like it could push or pull anything on wheels.

Many Dodges got a postwar "beauty treatment" in the late '50s and even gained tailfins in the beautiful Sweptside series. For the most part, the Power Wagon remained the Dodge chosen for wrecker duty.

During this era, four-wheel-drive versions of regular Dodge trucks also began to be called Power Wagons. The W300M designation was used to differentiate the original. The "M" suffix meant "military style."

In the late '50s and into 1960, Dodge truck sales skidded but they began to move up with a plain-looking but rugged new model in 1961. The D500 heavy-duty 1 1/2 -ton became a hit with towing professionals. Facelifts and cosmetic changes marked the late '60s Dodges.

Handsomely modernized in 1972, Dodge trucks seemed larger, more powerful and more rugged than their competitors. The illusion helped sales grow. These three factors counted a lot when a tower needed to update or expand the fleet.

By the 1980s, Dodge helped its sales by promoting its chassis-cab models as "Road Ready" trucks that could be equipped with factory-installed work bodies. One of these was the pretty and practical Dodge Retriever tow truck package.

The complete history of Dodge trucks in the '90s and 2000s still is being written. Towing professionals who are "in the know" say Dodge is up to the challenge of meeting the needs of the new millennium. They look forward to seeing the company's tow vehicles of the future.

Dodge's "Ram-Tough" commercial vehicles for 1985 included the Retriever tow-truck version of the chassis-and-cab model. It has a factory-installed work body. Dodge was the only truck maker offering such models directly from the assembly line. (Dodge News)

"RED DOG:" THE VINTAGE OLD PRO FROM PRO-TOW

By Tom Collins

Tim Rudolph and his showpiece 1968 Dodge WD 300 Power Wagon have something in common—their roots began serving the towing needs of people in the busy Cleveland, Ohio, area.

Both have migrated northwest to Hackensack, Minnesota, a beautiful lake country community midway between Duluth and Fargo, North Dakota.

The Dodge is the calling-card and showpiece of the business Tim and his wife, Jennie, have built in Hackensack.

Tim acquired the '68 Dodge from his former employer, Bud Martinowski, of North Olmstead, Ohio. It's a constant reminder of Bud who helped Tim get into the towing business.

At one time, the Dodge plowed snow at Cleveland's Hopkins International Airport.

In addition to an 8-foot snow plow, the Dodge is fitted with a 12,000 lb. winch, an 8,000 lb. boom winch, a four-speed PTO, a large aluminum tool box as well as a light bar, receiver hitch and jumper unit. It came with a variety of repair manuals.

Tim thought the frame and mechanical portions of the truck were in excellent condition but decided the body needed some work. He got in touch with Vintage Power Wagon of Fairfield, Iowa, to talk about restoration. Pro-Tow

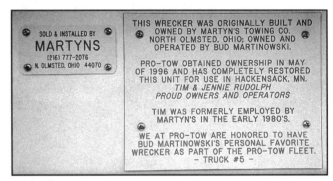

The "Red Dog," a restored 1968 Dodge, has two plaques affixed to it that detail its original Ohio heritage from Martyn's, North Olmstead, Ohio. It was original owner Bud Martinowski's favorite vehicle. (Tim and Jennie Rudolph)

Tim and Jennie Rudolph's "Red Dog" '68 Dodge Power Wagon was painted to match the other Pro-Tow fleet vehicles. It's used in parades and celebrations in Hackensack, Minnesota. (Tim and Jennie Rudolph)

employee Aaron Isaacs also contributed his thoughts about the eventual two-year restoration.

The rear quarter fenders were prefabricated with 1/4 inch steel for extra strength and durability.

A custom fabricated rear toolbox and running boards were made by L & M Steel of Brainerd, Minnesota. The truck's seat was reupholstered and North Lakes Auto and Marine of Hackensack painted the Dodge to match the rest of the Pro-Tow fleet, which includes four other wreckers and a tilt bed.

After plugging in Halogen lamps and fitting the Dodge with an aluminum exhaust system, the Rudolphs felt their great-looking veteran still needed an identity. It came from Tim's dad who supplied the hood ornament, a gold bulldog from a Mack.

"We nicknamed this wrecker 'Red Dog,'" says Jennie. "It's the one we use in parades and as a showpiece."

Tim began working with two trucks in 1974 at a

Corvette center in Syracuse, New York. Later, he managed a Shell station in North Olmstead, then worked at Martyn's Towing Service and later, a Marathon Service Center.

In 1985, he helped his parents move to Stoney Lake, Minnesota. Tim liked the area. There he fell in love and married Jennie in 1990.

After working in Stoney Lake, he began his own repair business from his home and soon bought a used wrecker from North Ridgeville, Ohio. (That's the same community that once was serviced by the Gilder family's towing and repair service.)

The original home-based Rudolph business was famous for three dogs and two cats who entertained customers. Now Pro-Tow operates from a repair facility just north of Hackensack on Minnesota Highway 371.

If you're in north central Minnesota, you might see the "Red Dog." It's the one Rudolph family dog that doesn't wag its tail—it just pulls with all its Power Wagon might!

When snow is in the air, Pro-Tow's 1968 Dodge Power Wagon "Red Dog" can double as a snow plow. It used to plow snow at Cleveland's Hopkins International Airport. (Tim and Jennie Rudolph)

FEDERAL
A FEDERAL CASE

By John Gunnell

Many civilian tow trucks have been based on Federal trucks. Federal produced a famous World War II heavy-duty wrecker as well. Until 1955, Federal Motor Truck Company was headquartered in Detroit, Michigan. There, in 1910, Martin L. Pulcher formed a predecessor firm named Bailey Motor Truck Company and built his first truck. Soon it carried the Federal name.

The company's slogan, "Never an Experiment," could have mirrored its conservative approach to truck building over 50 years. Federal assembled trucks from parts made by other companies. Tested, quality parts instead of new designs assured a durable product with proven engineering strengths.

As early as 1913 Federal produced 25 trucks for the U.S. Postal Service. Post office orders helped Federal reach total production of 1,000 trucks by the time it was three years old. Later, units were turned out for military use in World War I. By the late teens, Federals ranged from 1-1/2- to 7-ton models, plus tractors for pulling semi-trailers. By its 10th birthday, Federal announced it had made 27,017 trucks and added 18- and 25-passenger buses to its line.

With the tow truck industry in its infancy in 1927, Federal graduated from using the four-cylinder engines it had relied on for years to using a seven main bearing Continental six-cylinder engine.

The result was a number of new models in the 1- to 3-ton range that were very suitable for wrecker use. About the same time, Federal switched to vacuum-operated four-

Paul Martin's 1929 Federal wrecker put in an appearance at the 1990 Wally Rank Car Show in Milwaukee, Wisconsin. (OCW)

wheel hydraulic brakes that came in especially handy when towing disabled cars.

Paul Martin Incorporated, a Wisconsin firm, often brought a 1929 Federal Six tow truck to Milwaukee-area car shows. This fully-restored enclosed-cab truck had a push-type front bumper, an express body and a single-boom towing apparatus.

Federal truck styling seemed to follow the general lines of GMC trucks. This probably was a plus, especially after 1929, when General Motors developed its Art & Colour studio and applied industrial design concepts to automobiles and trucks.

In 1934, one-piece windshields and V-type radiators were seen on Federals. A year later, they showed streamlining influences with their V-shaped windshields, skirted fenders and horizontal hood louvers. Federal's very first cab-over-engine models evolved in 1937 and reflected an industry-wide revival of this style, which had been experimented with prior to 1920.

Streamlined cab-over-engine models, especially short-wheelbase units, gained some degree of popularity with towers in this era and provided operators with greater maneuverability at accident scenes. The additional Federal lines helped boost sales totals to as many as 4,000 trucks per year.

The Federal lineup, including the especially handsome conventional models, ranged from pickups to 6-ton heavies and offered plenty of models for tow-service operators to select.

In 1941, Thomas R. Lippard, founder of the Stewart Motor Corporation of Buffalo, N.Y., became Federal's third president. As World War II began, Lippard secured some lucrative government contracts. Federal produced the Model C-2, a large 7-1/2-ton 6 x 6 military aircraft wrecker.

Like the similar Jeeps made by Willys-Overland and Ford Motor Company, the giant C-2s were based on a generic government design and produced by Federal, Biederman and Reo. Federal designated their C-2 as Model 606. Later versions of the 606 were designated as C or D

Tom Ratliff's Federal C2 was a military tow truck before working in "civilian life" for a North Carolina towing service. It's now being restored. (Thomas Ratliff)

models and featured changes in both appearance and specifications.

Federal's early C-2s were built in the 1941-1942 era. Their headlights were mounted about 18 inches above the front bumper and carried a brush guard in front of the radiator grille.

A 1942 Federal press release boasted the 606 could pick up a medium bomber with ease and that two Federals working together could "swing the heaviest warplane now in production without a quiver or groan." The trucks had a 189.5-inch wheelbase, were 33-feet 9-inches long, including the tow boom, and stood 125 inches above the ground. Early versions of this 28,000-pound truck carried a curved 10-ton Gar Wood crane.

Federal-made C-2s had distinctions such as 8-segment hood louvers that made them look like the company's heavy-duty civilian models. They featured a 180-hp Hercules HXD L-head six-cylinder engine and a five-speed Spicer manual transmission plus a Wisconsin T-77-3 transfer case that gave 10 forward speeds. Cleveland Pneumatic air springs were used up front.

The wrecker was designed to pull a 40-foot long C-2 trailer where a disabled aircraft could be set.

Later versions of Federal's 606 (C-2) wrecker carried an 8-foot, straight-boom 5-ton Gar Wood crane that could telescope to 18, 22 or 26 feet. These Federal 606 models had built-in radiator and headlight brush guards.

After World War II, surplus C-2 Federals found their way into the hands of towing service operators across the country where some still are on the job!

Early postwar Federals exhibited few product changes. By 1951, the seller's market evaporated and updated models became a necessity. All-new Styleliner 1800 conventionals were introduced, along with a new, Federal-built "Power Chief" overhead-valve six-cylinder engine that produced 145 hp.

Despite the changes, Federal sales slipped from more than 6,000 in 1947 to only 874 in 1954. That low number included a very unusual "tow" truck specially built for the U.S. Air Force. Its crew cab was made by welding two GMC cabs back to back. The unusual cab was mounted high over the wheels, engine and hood.

During the mid-1950s, NAPCO Industries, Inc. purchased Federal and moved the headquarters to Minneapolis with production at Plymouth, Minnesota. NAPCO, which started as Northwest Auto Parts Company, did a lot of military production during World War II. In the '50s, it became a public company, changed its name and focused on making 4- and 6-wheel drive axle conversions and truck sanders.

Military orders and their new "Golden Eagle" civilian series barely kept Federal alive until 1959 when their last order of buses was shipped to Pennsylvania. There was some bus production for overseas markets but the Federal name was gone and their share of the tow truck business had vanished.

STYLISH FEDERAL STYLE LINER IS A '50s ROCKER By Tom Collins

Roger Heinbach has a 1950s gem among his truck collection in Idaho. The 1951 Federal Style Liner tow truck is as original as Chuck Berry, the Hula Hoop and "American Bandstand."

"It runs like a new truck and the paint is original," says Roger.

In 1951, the Federal dealer traveled to Detroit by train to pick up the completed wrecker from the Ashton company, makers of the tow boom and wrecker body. There is just 40,000 miles on its odometer today.

Powered by a Hercules six-cylinder engine, it has a five-speed transmission and two-speed rear axle. This Federal also featured swing-up front fenders for easier service.

Note the chrome grille, hood ornament and hood strip, cowl trim spear and curved one-piece windshield. Extras that add the '50s touch are the roof-mounted red bubble light, twin spotlights and wrecker body trim rail. Covered rear wheels add to the '50s look.

The silver streaked hood is somewhat like the era's Pontiacs. (Roger Heinbach)

After World War II, Federal produced a sculpted series of trucks. This '51 Styleliner tow truck is a rare example. (Roger Heinbach)

FORD MODEL AA FORD TOW TRUCK

By John Gunnell

Ford Motor Company's 25th anniversary – in 1928 – took place during what was undoubtedly the firm's most significant year in two decades. After 20 years of building and selling its spindly Model T, Ford was ready to launch an all-new model that was appropriately promoted as the "New Ford."

One tradition that wasn't broken was doubling the model designation to name the truck counterpart of the new vehicle. For example, the commercial version of the Model T had been called the TT, so the commercial version of the 1928 "New Ford" was called the Model AA.

Like Ford's new car, the truck version was powered by a sturdy 200.5-cid L-head four-cylinder engine that produced 40 hp at 2200 rpm and 128 lbs.-ft. of torque at 1,000 rpm.

Small Model A "trucks" — such as the pickup and panel — were car-based. In fact, they were actually known as "commercial cars." These vehicles were not up to big jobs such as hauling freight, carrying coal or towing the huge passenger cars of the era. On the other hand, the Model AA was a genuine 1-1/2-ton truck. Ford offered it with a full-range of job-rated bodies and heavy-duty accessories.

The Model AA truck did make use of the passenger car's radiator, cowl, hood, front fenders and headlight bar. It even came with a black-painted version of the car's bright metal radiator shell. Beyond that, it was bigger and stronger with its 113-1/2-in. wheelbase, a more massive frame, strong 13- or 16-leaf springs, 20-in. welded steel wheels and a 6-brake chassis with truck-type high-pressure tires. The Model AA also featured a two-piece drive shaft, larger radius rods and a hefty worm-gear rear axle. A stump-pulling dual-high transmission could also be ordered to provide six speeds forward and two in reverse.

To promote the 1928 Model AA to tow service operators, Ford took a closed-cab chassis and had it fitted with a custom-built high-side express body and a hoist, as well as headlamps and a nickel-plated radiator. This truck was photographed outside the company headquarters in Highland Park, Mich., and is believed to have been a prototype for the Ford dealer service trucks that appeared soon thereafter.

Featuring two-tone finish with Gunmetal Blue bodies and shiny black running gear, the "blue oval" service trucks were designed to give Ford dealers an "all-Ford" image. They drove home to the public the company's "we-service-what-we-sell" program. The actual Model AA dealer service trucks lacked the prototype's bright-finished radiator and headlight buckets, but they did come with bright metal rails atop the sides of the service body.

The fancy factory jobs were, of course, rarely indicative of what a hard-working Model AA tow truck might look like in real life. Most of these rigs were on the road daily yanking cars out of ditches, dragging in wrecks and providing 24-hour road service. Shiny paint, straight body panels and wash-ups were not as important as getting the

All American Towing of Mankato, Minnesota, uses this Model AA Ford wrecker to promote business. This photo was taken at a truck show by the late truck historian Robert Gary. (Robert Gary)

A 1929 Model AA Ford carries a homemade wrecker body that is a bit wider than most commercial bodies. (OCW)

job done when it needed doing.

Since Henry Ford never threw away a part he could sell, the point of transition from the 1928 Model AA to the 1929 edition is hard to determine with absolute certainty. Some trucks were built with parts from each of the years, but it is recorded that new six-hole ventilated disc wheels are one change that took place in February 1929. In October, a number of important mechanical upgrades were done and balloon tires became optional in January.

The third of the four years of Model A production was 1930, but it wasn't until the middle of that year — June 9 to be exact — that the truck line made news by adapting the 1930 passenger car's somewhat heftier appearance and adding a series of larger truck models on a 157-in. wheelbase.

No one knows if Henry Ford expected the Model A to last as long as the Model T did with only minimal changes, but things surely didn't work out that way. The times and vehicle-buying habits had changed. People were starting to look forward to annual new model changeovers. That meant more than a vehicle getting a minor facelift every 12 months.

While the 1931 Model A trucks looked much like the 1930 models, there were a number of new body styles added to the line and one of them was of particular interest to towing service operators. The Type 229-A was a closed-cab Service Car for the standard 131-1/2-in. wheelbase truck chassis. It featured a built-in tool chest and a mechanical hoist for just $715 over the price of the bare chassis.

According to company records, Ford purchased 521 of these "tow truck" bodies in 1931, hoping to sell them all to Model A buyers. However, the company then decided to halt production of Model AAs (as well as A's) at the end of the year. When this was done, the Type 229-A body was removed from the sales catalog offerings, although Ford continued installing the leftover bodies on later-model Ford V-8 chassis until all the bodies were gone.

Today, if you're looking for a tow truck from the 1920s or 1930s to restore, there's a very good chance that you might run across a Model AA in your search. These trucks are very good looking, popular with collectors and sturdy enough to survive the passing of seven decades of time.

Model AA Ford wreckers were used around the world. This one was used by E. G. Lange, A/B, Uddevalla, Sweden. (Anders Willegard)

Bruce L. Palmer of Canal Winchester, Ohio, owns this well-preserved Ford Model AA tow truck which appears to be factory-made 229-A body wrecker. (Bruce L. Palmer)

IT'S EASY TO GET "HOOKED" ON FORD TOW TRUCKS

By John Gunnell

Some people think that Henry Ford invented the automobile. Although it's not true, Ford was a pioneer in the automaking industry. There is confusion about who invented the first tow truck, but there's sufficient fact to suggest Ford pioneered this field, too, if it wasn't the first.

For years, tow truck historians debated the claims of two companies who say they created the first tow truck. Both the Manley Manufacturing Co. of Hanover, Pa., and the Holmes Co., of Chattanooga, Tenn., long ago advertised each had originated the auto wrecking crane.

The Volunteer State outfit credited its founder, Ernest W. Holmes, Sr., with developing his crane "from local use in 1915." It is established fact the first production-type Holmes vehicle hoist came in 1916. The Keystone State company says its device was "first offered to dealers and garagemen of this country by Robert E. Manley in 1917.

A third manufacturer, Ashton Equipment Co., of Dearborn, Mich. — Ford Motor Company's hometown — waited until 1969 to claim it had built the first "real" tow truck. An Ashton advertisement in the May 5, 1969 issue

of Automotive News showed one of the firm's wrecker units mounted on a Ford Model TT truck in 1916. This pinpoints Ford as a towing pioneer and may vindicate the view that the first genuine purpose-built tow truck (not just a wrecking crane) was a Ford.

A look at the Crestline Series book Wreckers and Tow Trucks by Donald F. Wood, indicates many Model Ts—from roadsters used as dealer service cars and pickups with tilting A-frame hoists to larger TT trucks with parallel-I-beam type hoists—were used to provide emergency road and wrecker service to motorists suffering highway mishaps.

Two very interesting photos in the book's first chapter show adaptations of other types of Fords to towing operations.

In Wood's first photo, a Model TT tilt-bed dump truck was used to move a Model T touring car with a damaged front axle. The dump box was tilted so the front end of the car could be supported. The car was fastened to the dump box and hauled with the box in raised position. The second picture shows a Model T turtle-deck roadster modified to

This tow truck show featured two vintage Fords, a postwar F-series (left) owned by Andy's Towing and a Model AA wrecker (right) owned by All American Towing of Mankato, Minnesota. (Bob Gary)

George Kaiser, Glenolden, Pennsylvania, displayed his 1953 Ford F-500 wrecker in Class 22F at the Antique Automobile Club of America's Fall National Meet at Hershey, Pennsylvania, several years ago.(John Gunnell)

tow a Model T touring car. The roadster has been fitted with a chassis extension and a "fifth-wheel" arrangement for towing. A man who sent this photograph to Automotive News in 1969 said the towing setup had been fabricated by Fred R. Baker, owner of a Ford garage in Brandon, Vermont.

Fords gained some popularity as service cars and wreckers in the 1930s. To understand why, we have to take a look at the towing industry of those days. At that time, a large number of independent garagemen couldn't afford a factory-built tow truck, but most were handy enough to cut the body of a classic car and mount a hoist in the rear. The result was a cheap towing rig with the sturdiness and pulling power of a new 1-ton wrecker.

Like the Ford trucks themselves, many of the hoists mounted to them were takeoffs or home-fabricated. It didn't make sense to pay $250 or $300 for a crane from Weaver, Little Giant or Manley to install on a $50 wrecker. A $600 cable-rigged Holmes with adjustable booms was out of the question. Often, the parts for the hoist came from the scrap pile and consisted of old car frame rails bolted in A-frame style and fitted with pulleys, chains and a crank.

Other garages simply mounted "speed hoists" they used to yank engines from a hook on the boom. When the towing was done, the hoist could be reattached to the shop's ceiling to do double duty.

These home-fabricated tow trucks were fine for gypsy grease monkeys hauling cars out of the ditch in Tooterville, but weren't long on eye appeal. Garages with image concerns or new-car dealers concerned about drawing in hard-to-find buyers needed a compromise.

The makers of smaller, (up to 1-ton) lower-priced trucks like Ford, Chevrolet and Dodge were the answer. They provided a well-outfitted road service truck with a wrecker crane and body, towing tools and equipment, custom paint and even insurance for $1,200-$1,500.

Naturally, a dealer selling Ford or Lincoln automobiles preferred a Ford wrecker. In the 1930s, the home office provided dealers with a loose-leaf style Truckfax book from which they could commission a rig through factory-approved aftermarket firms. Two suppliers of wrecker bodies were listed in Truckfax.

Chicago Crane and Engineering Co. offered their wrecker crane, which weighed 400 lbs. and sold for $95. It included 35 feet of 1/2-in. cable, snatch blocks, a positive ratchet and dual cranks. A sheave pulley was provided to permit double- and triple-pull operation and to give quadruple purchase when extra power was necessary.

Ford Motor Co. also approved three Weaver wrecker bodies. Two were hand-crank models priced at $85 and $110 respectively. The third was powered by a 2-hp engine and sold for $390. Weaver units came with two drums holding 300 ft. of cable. The drums could be operated separately or in tandem. The lower drum also could be rigged to pull as a level winch.

As the effects of the Depression in America began to ease a bit, Ford applied some style to its dealer service truck designs and even offered a special high-side express body with chrome bed rails manufactured by Briggs Body Co. Adorned with the blue-oval badge and Ford script logo and frequently dressed-up with two-tone paint, whitewall tires, wheel trim rings, diamond plate moldings and triple front bumpers (chrome-plated of course!) these handsome rigs gave many Ford dealerships a snappy, professional look.

Successful private operators were just as likely as dealers to use lower-priced, purpose-built tow trucks. Across the tops of pages 66-67 of Wood's book there is a panoramic photo of approximately 32 vehicles owned by companies that had road service contracts with the Missouri Auto Club in 1934.

"Fords and Chevrolets were most prevalent," the author notes.

Although we have no statistics to prove it, photos in books and archives suggest that from the late '30s through the early '50s, tow trucks generally got bigger. This would be logical because of many factors.

While the giant classic cars were vanishing, the typical family car was getting bigger and heavier, making towing more of a chore. Roads also were getting bigger and more suitable to high-speed driving. This all led to more devastating accident scenes.

The trucks carried more equipment and tools and had to be larger. And part of this era was the increased military-vehicle production—with much of the post-war surplus hardware finding its way to tow-truck operators.

We see photos of Ford trucks that are more in the 1-1/2-ton and up range than lighter capacities. Streamlined cab-over-engine (COE) models seem like they were particularly suited to towing service because of their greater maneuverability. Ford continued to offer the handsome service-truck body with chrome bed rails, but it curved downwards at the rear as streamlining came into vogue. Wider rear fenders were provided for the dual-rear-wheel arrangements so vital in wrecker operations where traction was more important than raw power. Ford Marmon-Herrington four-wheel-drive conversions also became more common.

The early postwar era brought an economic boom and a trend toward suburban living that created a demand for more gas stations and service garages. As these businesses enjoyed success due to the nation's growing prosperity, many expanded into the towing service field. Developments like the overhead-valve V-8 engine, automatic transmission, factory-built four-wheel-drive models and power-assisted accessories meant smaller tow trucks could do more and became more convenient to use. They were less expensive to purchase and were easier to store in neighborhood filling stations or repair shops.

Trucks of 1/2-ton to 1-1/2-ton capacities fitted with optional "dualies" became the standard of the industry in this era. Ford's famous F-series models of the '50s and '60s provided 24-hour towing services in hamlets and villages from coast to coast.

By the late '60s and early '70s, there was a trend, started by Dodge, to merchandise some tow truck bodies for

This F-250 Styleside pickup with wrecker equipment was illustrated in the 1960 Ford "4-Wheel-Drive" sales folder. Four-wheel-drive models provided power-take-off points on the transfer case to drive winches and other equipment. (OCW)

"heavy" versions of light-duty trucks direct from the factory.

A reversal in trends came with the gas crisis of the mid-'70s, when supply problems and price fluctuations led to the closing of many independent gas stations. The towing business began to trend more towards specialized operators and higher-technology mounted on ever-larger truck chassis that could handle a variety of jobs. Towing equipment makers have consolidated to the point where new brands are dominating the market and some of the old brands are built on the same assembly lines, though merchandised through different dealers.

Some older Ford tow trucks are finding their way into the hands of car collectors. While the collector appeal of the full-size rigs naturally is limited to those with room to store them (as well as experience with fixing and using them) there are many instances in which a collector car might need a push or a pull. One of the neatest sights at an old car show is seeing a Ford collector bring his Model A to the meet on the back of a Model AA wrecker.

We might mention that toy versions of Ford tow trucks are showing up regularly these days and apparently selling quite well. There is interest in both toys made years ago and those being turned out today.

In some cases, the contemporary miniatures are being re-issued with different colors and markings to keep collectors supplied with "new products" derived from the same basic model.

If you get the urge to purchase a real Ford tow truck that's in its "senior" years, the first place to look is in the truck section of the **Old Cars Weekly** classifieds. To subscribe or for more information, contact:

Old Cars Weekly
700 East State Street
Iola, Wisconsin 54990
(800)-258-0929

Magazines published by organizations like the Antique Truck Historical Society, P.O. Box 901611, Kansas City, MO 64190-1611, the Antique Truck Club of America, P.O. Box 97, Apollo, PA 15613 and Vintage Truck, P.O. Box 838, Yellow Springs, OH 45387 may also carry vintage tow truck ads. Once in awhile, an older model will also pop up for sale in towing industry publications.

The 1967 Ford sales catalog showed a Bronco with a tow crane and push bumper attending a very airbrushed station wagon. (OCW)

A BRIEF HISTORY
OF PRE-WORLD WAR II
FORD WRECKERS

By John Gunnell

The earliest Ford tow truck shown in Jim Wagner's excellent book *Ford Trucks since 1905* (Crestline, 1978) is a 1920 Model TT wrecker that carries the name of S and L Motor Co. Lettering on the truck indicates this Ford franchise was on Wabash Ave., probably in the Chicago area.

The 1920 Model TT truck has a "circus truck" look with its light-colored paint and fancy lettering. Its enclosed cab was an after-market item—Ford Motor Co. didn't offer a "factory" enclosed cab until the spring of 1925. The truck's platform body carries a large cable reel that stretches to the towing boom. The cable winds onto a spool made of Model T wood-spoke wheels. The body rises in round shapes, on each side, to cover the spoke wheels. It's probably among the earliest Ford wreckers.

Wagner points out the 1-ton Model TT was introduced

O. D. Electric Service of California used this restored 1932 Ford Model BB wrecker. It appears to be a 1-ton chassis but without the high-sided Ford factory service body. (Jim Gustafson)

in 1917 starting at $600. It was a Model T car with a stretched 124-in. wheelbase, an over-slung worm-gear rear axle and 32 x 3-1/2-in. solid-rubber tires. The "TT" designation stood for "T Truck" or "Ton Truck."

Wagner's book jumps to a custom-built, 1928 tow-truck beauty. It's a company-owned, special-bodied Model AA. It was the 1-ton version of the Model A car, which replaced the Model T in 1928. The tow truck is parked in front of FoMoCo's old headquarters in Highland Park, Michigan.

It looks like a large pickup with a small grain-box body and a hoist. Wagner believes this truck was the prototype for the beautiful Type 229-A body that was used in building official Ford Dealer Service Cars. The prototype had split running board aprons, a nickel radiator and brightly chromed headlamps.

Ford's handsome factory-issued Service Cars had high-side cargo boxes with chrome box rails and a curved, hand-operated hoist. The majority of production models had one-piece running board aprons, painted headlamps and black-finished radiator shells. Wagner notes the tow truck used in a photo wasn't done in Ford's standard Gunmetal-Blue truck color. It featured a Ford script embossed above its rear cab window.

Though eye appealing, the service trucks did not sell well. Ford produced only 521 Type 229-A bodies in 1931, before removing the Model AA from production. Finished Service Cars were ordered so infrequently, some of the bodies weren't used for at least three years. The company mounted them on later-model, V-8-powered Ford truck

chassis since Henry Ford didn't believe in waste or obsolescence.

Wagner's book also shows a nice '31 Model AA Ford with optional dual rear wheels pulling a styled trailer loaded with a 1930 Fordson tractor. This rig was operated by Tynan-Alexander Motors Ltd. and had bright-metal trim on the headlamp buckets and radiator shell. The metal rails that top the bed sides extend to the rear step plate, like those on old fire trucks.

The basic configuration of the 1-ton Ford tow truck essentially stayed the same over the next few years, often with old factory bodies fitted to a newer chassis. The Model T lasted nearly 20 years and the Model A stuck around for four years. Newer Ford trucks revealed their cosmetic appearance changes every year or two.

Ford's major technical advance was the release of a V-8 engine in 1932, offered in cars first and trucks late in the year. With 65-hp, it finally gave the 1-ton Ford wrecker a little pulling power to spare.

Wagner's book also shows a 1934 wrecker operated by the Dawson-Long Ford garage. The lettering shows Linwood Ave. and a Euclid 4982 phone number, which sounds like New York City to this native. This V-8-powered Ford has the old 229-A body adapted to the 131.5-in. wheelbase Model BB running gear. Its optional dual wheels carry Goodyear 6.50 x 20 tires. In the depths of the Depression, June 6, 1934, Ford's BB 1-ton truck was reduced to $755.

A 1939 Ford. It illustrates the new Model 99T 1-1/2-

A 1934 Ford V-8 carried what appeared to be a homemade tow unit. It was for sale at an auto show for just $1,750. (OCW)

ton chassis with this era's streamlined service truck body. The basic truck had a rounded hood, fenders and cab. The high-sided service body looked like an upside-down row boat viewed from the side. The "bow" curved down to the rear bumper. This truck rode a 134-in. wheelbase chassis. It was available with an 85-hp V-8 for $675 or the bigger 95-hp V-8 for $700. The factory-style two-tone paint job was darker on the hood, cab and running boards.

The last pre-war tow truck in Wagner's book is a 1941 Ford service truck on the 1-ton chassis with snow tires. Its wide, arched towing crane overhangs the rear of the vehicle. In May 1941, the smaller 221-cid flathead V-8 was rated at 90-hp and 150 lb.-ft. of torque. The larger 239-cid V-8 got a higher torque rating. A six was added to the line

for some trucks, but it's likely that most — if not all — towing services preferred a V-8.

Wagner was educated as a mechanical engineer and went to work for Ford in 1963. Eight years later, he moved to the light-truck engineering department. His book reflects a deep, consuming passion for the commercial vehicles Ford built between 1905 and 1978. It has been reprinted unchanged several times. It is now marketed by Classic Motorbooks of Osceola, Wis., which bought Crestline Publishing Co. some years ago. It sells for about $40, but you can find older editions at flea markets for less and they cover the same history.

Rudy Dud's Body Shop used what appears to be a 1934 Ford wrecker to "hook" this early 1980s Ford sedan that was involved in an accident. Many people only see towing equipment at the worst times. (OCW)

GRADE "AA" OPERATIONS

By John Gunnell

Patrick Gilliam has been active in the towing business since 1970 and judging from the two antique tow trucks he uses for promotional purposes, his business is "Grade AA" all the way. One of the restored trucks that advertises Gilliam's Military Towing Service of Niagara Falls, New York, is a stock 1928 Model AA Ford. The other is a 1929 Model AA street rod tow truck that was custom-built from an original Ford tow truck fitted with a Holmes wrecker.

Patrick's restored-as-original truck represents the first year of the Model AA Ford truck's history. Its 200.5-cid flathead four-cylinder engine produces 40-hp at 2200 rpm and 128 lbs.-ft. of torque at 1,000 rpm. Like other Model AA trucks, it carries a 1-1/2-ton rating. The AA trucks were marketed with a full range of job-rated bodies and heavy-duty accessories.

The AA truck shared the legendary Model A Ford passenger car's front-end sheet metal and featured a painted version of the classic car's bright metal radiator shell (although Patrick's truck has been restored with a deluxe style, chrome radiator). Naturally, the Ford truck was heftier than the Ford passenger car and rode on a 113-1/2-in. wheelbase. Other selling features included a massive frame, strong 13- or 16-leaf rear springs, 20-in. diameter welded steel wheels, a six-brake chassis, truck-type high-pressure tires, a two-piece drive shaft, larger radius rods and a hefty worm-gear rear axle. An optional Dual-High transmission provided six forward speeds and two reverse gears.

Patrick's truck is finished in shiny black with red pin striping. Behind the cab is a wooden platform and an original oak tool box. The truck carries a circa-1920s Manley crane mounted on a piece of polished diamond plate. It also features a hand winch, a drag winch and distance bar—all by Manley. The vintage towing apparatus is finished in bright red to match the truck's bright red wheels, which are fastened with bright metal lug nuts.

With an equally bright appearance, Patrick's second truck is a clear reflection of the art of street rodding at its best. The 1929 Model AA wrecker is powered by a heavily chromed, up-to-date V-8 engine. The body is lowered all around and rides on ventilated chrome disc wheels wearing skinny tires up front and fat drag slicks at the rear.

The hot rod hauler's bright red finish is set off against black fenders and running boards. The radiator grille, headlamps, tie-bar and horns are all chrome plated. The bed of the truck sports a polished diamond-plate liner and bright metal bed rails adorn the sidewalls. The Holmes crane is also done in black, as is the exterior roof on the truck's cab.

"We meet by accident" is the slogan used by Military Towing Service, but it's probably no accident that the business is a big success. After all, those antique trucks serve as a great advertising tool and generate extra customers. Military Towing Service offers 24-hour service. The company is associated with the American Automobile Association (AAA), Amoco and the Allstate Motor Club.

The business view of this 1928 Ford Model AA is equipped with a tow crane, hand winch, drag winch and distance bar—all built in the 1920s by Manley. (Patrick Gilliam)

Patrick Gilliam of Niagara Falls, New York, owns this Model AA Ford that represents the first year of that series production, 1928. (Patrick Gilliam)

IT'S THE TOW TRUCK VERSION OF A "3-in-1" KIT!

By Tom Collins

Pete's Auto Repair of Waupun, Wisconsin, has an interesting 1950 Ford F-7 tow truck available for the right buyer. Like those classic AMT "3-in-1" model kits, the veteran Ford was put together from portions of two and possibly three truck choices.

The cab, hood and fenders were taken from a great looking Ford F-7 that spent much of its work life as a fire truck. The working end is a Holmes 500 wrecker, a classic example of equipment from the '50s. It all rides on a Marmon-Herrington platform, Ford's source of four-wheel-drive components.

The Ford was carefully pieced together by John Kubiak of Green Bay, Wisconsin, who kept the truck for several years. Current owner Pete Lawrie of Waupun, Wisconsin, is reluctantly selling the F-7 after enjoying it for more than seven years.

"The wrecker was used to advertise Pete's Auto Repair and Sales. It's pretty big to store but I don't want it sitting outside," Pete says.

Pete is nostalgic about the big Ford because it reminds him of one owned by Stam Auto Body of Waupun when he was growing up.

"My dad owned a service station and their Ford used to come in to get gas. I'd stand on the running board and look at the tool box and the boom. I was always interested in wreckers as a kid."

Pete wants the Ford to have a good, caring home. He witnessed an original '33 Ford wrecker that deteriorated over the years and doesn't want that to happen to his F-7.

Pete's Auto Repair, Waupun, Wisconsin, was selling this 1950 Ford F-7 tow truck. It is a Ford set over a chassis with Marmon-Herrington all wheel drive chassis and gearbox. (John Gunnell)

The 1950 Ford was one of the "Bonus Built" series originally introduced in 1948. Ford promised a truck that would last 10 years which brought a lot of attention in that era.

The most notable upgrade for the average person is what Ford called the "Million Dollar Cab." Its larger doors and taller cab featured increased headroom and what Ford called "living room comfort."

Also included was an adjustable seat on a track for more legroom. Coil seat springs and extra cotton stuffing helped make the driver much more comfortable. Better suspension and insulation were meant to free drivers and passengers from engine/ chassis vibrations. The new cab styling also offered improved ventilation.

The "Bonus Built" Ford series also introduced a saying that would last longer than 10 years: "Built stronger to last longer."

The F-7 models used a 336.7-cid flathead V-8 that produced 145-hp at 3600 rpm. The Ford "E" series V-8, with modifications, was used in that era's Lincolns. The truck V-8s produced 255 torque feet at 1800 rpm with a 3.50 bore, 4.375 stroke and a compression ratio of 6.4:1.

The pairing of a Ford with the Marmon-Herrington all-wheel-drive unit actually is a coupling of two very old companies. Marmon-Herrington's parent company was producing machinery for flour mills as far back as 1851.

In the 1930s, as interest in their Marmon cars waned, that company joined forces with an engineer named Arthur Herrington to begin building military and large commercial vehicles. Soon Ford's truck division partnered with Marmon-Herrington to convert selected models to all-wheel-drive trucks.

The Marmon-Herrington Fords generally carry a separate oval badge on their hoods displaying that heritage in addition to their "blue oval" Ford identity.

Original Ford Marmon-Herringtons also had tags inside the cab with the 5-speed and auxiliary shift pattern diagrams. The tag warns: "Bring truck to full stop before shifting auxiliary transmission." Another tag usually indicates the vehicle is a Ford converted to all-wheel-drive by Marmon-Herrington of Indianapolis, Indiana.

Pete's "3-in-one-kit" Ford sports a Holmes 500 wrecker unit and accessories from the era. It has a large tool box, chains, various blocks and an old lighting unit.

"Everything on it may seem primitive by today's standards, but this unit really was the best when it was new," says Pete.

"When I began working there was a '37 International in town with a hand-cranked winch and an old metal bar that attached to the car being towed. That seemed primitive to me."

Pete's Ford is a reminder of the hard working tow trucks that served small towns and large cities alike as Americans took to the highways in ever-increasing numbers following WWII.

He's hoping this classic "3-in-1" will bring joy to the next collector as it has to Pete and his business.

This 1950 Ford has a higher profile because of its Marmon-Herrington all-wheel-drive chassis. It carries a Holmes 500 tow unit. (John Gunnell)

FWD WORKING ON THE RAILROAD

By John Gunnell

When a car blows a tire, the owner might call a Chevy, Ford or Dodge tow truck for tire repairs. When a semi-truck does the same, you call a towing service with a heavy-duty Navistar or Kenworth wrecker. So, who do you call when a railcar suffers wheel problems? How about the FWD Corp. of Clintonville, Wisconsin.?

This small company has made some of the best railroad-service trucks around. At least three types of such trucks can be classified as wreckers. The first is the "re-railer" designed to put derailed engines and cars back on their tracks. The second is the "wide-treader," which can be used to repair bridges or handle derailments. Last is the "wheel truck," which is used to bring replacement sets of

New York Central's 1961 FWD "wide treader" was a bridge-repair unit with an 81-in. straddle-track tread. (OCW)

flanged steel railcar wheels right to the car for on-site replacement.

A BACKGROUND IN RAILROADING

Perhaps FWD's link to railroading is natural. Back in 1905, when FWD co-founder Otto Zachow was busy inventing the ball-and-socket joint that became the basis of the four-wheel-drive principle, his son worked as an apprentice machinist at the Chicago Northwestern Railroad shop in Fond du Lac, Wisconsin. That's where Otto took his invention when he wanted to have mechanical drawings of it created.

Some early FWD trucks were actually pressed into railroad duty as locomotives. In the 1920s, one FWD Model "B" truck was used as an engine for a short-line railroad in Louisiana. The New Orleans and Lower Coast

The Milwaukee Road used this FWD "Blue Ox" chassis for this "Sky Worker" unit. (Mark Wayman)

Road equipped the truck with flanged wheels and it replaced an old steam locomotive.

As late as 1947, a fleet of then-new FWDs was shipped to Chinese freedom fighter Sun Yat Sen. The trucks in the fleet were put to work as locomotives on the China National Railroad's Canton-to-Hengyang line. The FWD trucks pulled three standard 40-ft. boxcars as far as 450 miles.

The original use of FWD trucks in railroad service dates to a period right after World War I when many FWDs were returning from the battlefields of Europe. These frequently were sold as military-surplus equipment—in many cases, to railroads from various parts of the United States.

"RE-RAILERS"

In the early '60s, FWD pushed to generate railroad business. The company gave various kinds of trucks made for rail-service work exposure in its corporate magazine *FWD News*. One issue from 1960 or 1961 pictured the Chesapeake & Ohio Railroad's "Big Bertha." This was a straddle-track FWD carrier that achieved new mobility in the handling of derailments. FWD News reported that it "cut re-railing times for C & O."

The Rock Island Line in Illinois (made famous by a song) had a re-railer called the "Blue Ox." The Chicago & Northwestern Railroad had a "400" re-railer truck. Around the same time, FWD constructed similar trucks for the Northern Pacific Railroad and the Minneapolis & St. Louis Railway. The first was a COE truck with a Ford cab and the second was a conventional FWD with its trademark long-hood styling.

Both of these trucks carried a house-shaped structure of steel girders on a platform body. An overhead crane moved

The Northern Pacific Railroad's **FWD** mobile wrecker unit could travel on rail and highway, speeding equipment wherever it was needed. FWD bought Ford tilt cabs and adapted them for their specialty trucks. (Mark Wayman)

back and forth on a sturdy horizontal center beam.

The center beam hung over the back of the truck and, with the crane moved to the extreme rear of the beam, a heavy load (like a railcar) could be lifted onto the truck's platform. *FWD News* described these as "mobile wreckers," actually re-railers similar to "Big Bertha."

"WIDE TREADER"

Around 1960, FWD built a wide treader for the New York Central Railroad. This truck actually was designed as a bridge-repair unit with an 81-in. straddle-track tread. The crane on the back was the same basic design as Big Bertha's crane. The New York Central unit also had rear-mounted outriggers and could easily have been used to do re-railing jobs when it wasn't busy repairing bridges.

WHEEL TRUCKS

When railcars suffered "hot boxes" (axle or wheel damage), wheel trucks carried extra sets right to the train. Some wheel trucks could travel by rail or highway, such as an FWD unit made for Northern Pacific's Rail & Road. Others were designed for highway-only. By speeding sets of replacement wheels to cars on the line, the wheel trucks expedited the movement of freight loads and saved money for the railroads.

In 1962, the Atlantic Coast Line Railroad purchased an FWD six-wheeler "wheel truck" for its Waycross, Ga.

division. The railroad later commissioned construction of four brand new FWD "wheel trucks" to be placed along the railroad's right-of-way so each truck covered a 200-mile radius.

The four trucks were FWD Tractioneer three-axle six-wheel-drive units. All of their differentials could be locked for positive traction. These trucks could travel over all types of terrain. They had a top highway speed of 60 mph thanks to a 318.4-cid GMC 6V-53 diesel engine.

Each truck was equipped with a Type CP-125-RG2 air compressor and carried two mounted reels (each with 10-ft. of air hose), with quick disconnects and shut-off valves on each side of the vehicle. Five-ton articulating cranes with a 360-degree swing were mounted at the extreme rear of each truck. There were outriggers and controls on both sides of the crane.

A 20,000-lb. winch was located on the front of the truck, which also had an SAE power-take-off and mounted controls. There were air jacks plus many necessary tools and supplies such as brasses, knuckles and pins. The trucks could carry two or three extra pairs of railcar wheels. There also was welding equipment and floodlights. They could expedite the removal and reloading of freight directly at the railcar-accident scene.

Chesapeake and Ohio Railroad's "Big Bertha" was a conventional model FWD straddle-track carrier that achieved a high degree of mobility in handling derailments. (Mark Wayman)

GMC
1937 GMC TOW TRUCKS OFFERED STREAM-STYLE AND DUAL-TONE COLOR DESIGN

By John Gunnell

The totally-redesigned 1937 GMC trucks featured a new front-end look that the General Motors Truck Co. called "built-in" styling. The "torpedo" headlights were set in the fender valleys and new, "dual-tone" color designs appeared. The radiator grille combined three sections of horizontal bars with a broad center portion of bright vertical fins. There were 12 dual-tone paint options with the wheels, radiator surround and body beads done in a contrasting color.

Some lighter-duty tow trucks of this era were little more than modified pickup trucks. These models used an L-head Oldsmobile which was enlarged to a 3-7/8 x 4-1/8-in. bore and stroke. It displaced 229.7- cid and developed 86-hp at 3500 rpm and 172 lbs.-ft. of torque at 1,200 rpm.

Another popular platform for light tow truck use was the GMC 3/4-ton Model T-16L that featured the same styling changes seen on the smaller T-14, as well as the same six-cylinder Oldsmobile L-head engine. Other 1937 GMC trucks had the same engines they used in 1936,

except the biggest 1936 engine — a huge 450-cid six — was no longer offered.

GMC marketed a wide variety of both its long-hooded conventional models and its "stub-nose" cab-over-engine (COE) trucks in 1937. Each of these styles had useful features for vehicle-recovery professionals. The heaviest conventional was the 12-ton T-61H. The 3/4-ton F16 was the lightest COE, while the heftiest was the 12-ton F-61H. Chassis prices ranged up to $3,985 for conventional cab-behind-engine trucks and $4,355 for COEs. Back then adding a tow boom increased the price by just a few hundred dollars, but that was plenty in those early post-Depression years.

"The Truck of Value, GMC Cab-Over-Engine," said a 1937 advertisement showing a drawing of the front end of a 1-1/2-ton COE truck finished in bright yellow with red trim. "See GMC for extra value . . . for advances stream-style with exclusive 'dual-tone' color design . . . for half-ton trucks with either short or long wheelbases and the biggest

Kenworthy Truck and Auto Company of Sparta, Wisconsin, restored this 1937 conventional-cab GMC tow truck. It was shown at the Iola Old Car Show in July 2001. (Kenworthy Truck and Auto Repair)

bodies available . . . for either standard or cab-over-engine trucks ranging in capacity to 12-tons . . . for 'truck-built' trailers . . . for improvements and refinements that assure greater economy and improved performance . . . and for prices that are extremely low."

The ad also pointed out that buyers could take advantage of "time payments through our Yellow Manufacturing Acceptance Corp. plan at lowest available rates." (GMC had merged with John D. Hertz's Yellow Truck & Coach Co. and, technically, was operated as the manufacturing subsidiary of YT and C through 1943).

Calendar-year sales of 1937 GMC trucks crested at the 50,000 level for the first time. Ward's 1942 Automotive Yearbook estimated model-year production at 56,996 units. GMC was evolving into a major player in the manufacture of all truck classes and its growth brought new acquisitions. In April 1937, GMC purchased the Wilson Foundry and Machine Co. buildings on South Saginaw Street in Pontiac, Michigan. Those facilities were converted for use in the manufacture of GMC light-duty truck engines.

During 1937, GMC also was building up its business among towing service operators as it sought new customers. Although it didn't offer factory-built tow trucks, GMC provided the basic truck and worked with approved body builders and towing equipment makers to provide car dealers and garage operators with a range of sturdy and affordable recovery vehicles.

Kenworthy Truck & Auto Company, of Sparta, Wisconsin, restored the 1937 GMC tow truck shown in the accompanying photos.

This truck started its life as a 1-1/4-ton GMC chassis and cab with dual rear wheels. Its hand-cranked "Auto Backing Crane" was manufactured by Manley Manufacturing Co., which was a Division of the American Chain Company, Inc. The Manley Manufacturing Division later became known as ACCO.

Manley was a pioneer tow truck equipment maker. According to the data plate affixed to this particular crane, the firm had moved from Bridgeport, Connecticut, to York, Pennsylvania, by the time the unit was built. It was mounted on a wooden platform at the rear of the GMC and the "wrecker body" was constructed almost like a shallow pickup truck's bed. The special rear fenders were designed to cover the dual rear wheels.

The 1937 GMC carries a Manley "Auto Backing Crane" and advertises "24 Hour Towing." (John Gunnell)

The 1937 GMC, restored in tow truck trim, looks great in a natural setting. (OCW)

The handsome Kenworthy GMC was originally a farm truck and was shown as a flatbed at a past Iola Old Car Show. (Tom Collins)

GMC'S COE TRUCKS MADE GREAT "TOE" TRUCKS

By John Gunnell

After experimenting with some really ugly preliminary designs in the mid-1930s, the GMC truck branch of General Motors started offering a variety of strikingly handsome cab-over-engine (COE) trucks in 1937. The talented designers of the GM Art & Colour Section —the auto industry's first real styling studio — created them. These were known as the "F" or "FC" series for "Forward-Control." They made great tow trucks because they were hefty, but had a short wheelbase that gave them great maneuverability.

The F16 was the lightest COE, while the heftiest was the 12-ton F-61H. Prices ranged from $635 to $4,355 for these models. "The Truck of Value, GMC Cab-Over-Engine," said a 1937 advertisement showing a drawing of the front end of a 1-1/2-ton COE truck finished in bright yellow with red trim.

Totally new GMC models arrived in 1939. An "AC" prefix indicated conventional-cab trucks and an "AF" designation identified the COE or forward-control trucks. The main change to COE models was they got their own version of the "fish skeleton" grille seen on other 1939 GMC products.

By 1941, the AF models were re-designated as CFs. They came in a variety of weight ranges from 1-ton up. Short-wheelbase COE semi-tractors also were introduced for the first time, along with a complete line of six-wheel-drive models and special dump trucks. A six-cylinder diesel engine was put into production. That year, a radically new AY series of 3-1/2- to 5-ton COEs with set back front axles was introduced.

After this, few major changes were made, with the slowdown in innovations due mainly to the outbreak of World War II and the conversion of the production lines to military vehicle manufacturing. During 1946, the CF-300 COE series offered six 1-1/2-ton models. The AF-520 2-ton tractor line featured four models while the AFR-750 3-1/2-ton tractor line also had four models.

Two all-new series of postwar COE trucks in the 16,000-lb. GVW class were introduced in 1948. They were the FF-350, offering 10 models with wheelbases from 122 in. to 197 in. on a 1-1/2-ton chassis and the FF-450, a heavier version of the same line with a larger, more powerful 104-hp version of the GMC 270 six-cylinder engine.

For 1950, GMC continued to make a full assortment of COE models in the medium- and heavy-duty ranges. In addition to basic flatbeds, stakes and delivery models, they included highway tractors, dump trucks and, of course, tow trucks. One of these GMCs, a 1947 model, owned by

Lanser Towing Company of Belgium, Wisconsin, can be seen in the National Towing & Recovery Museum in Chattanooga, Tennessee.

Late in 1953, GMC introduced a new COE series styled under the supervision of General Motors design director Harley Earl. The new appearance was characterized by a snub-nosed look and rounded feature lines. Truck collectors have nicknamed these handsome haulers "cannonballs." They were also offered in 12 different colors available in five two-tone combinations.

Introduced on August 12, 1954 was a new "Stripway" system for COE trucks of 5-ton-and-up GVWS. It gave service personnel easier access to the engine, transmission and other components. Counter-balanced seats were used that slid up to the ceiling. This permitted engineers to incorporate fold-back floorboards and side doors that swung open on each side of the large hood.

Major styling changes for 1955 were most apparent on the trucks in GMC's medium- and heavy-duty model ranges. The 550 and 650 models, with GCWs up to 55,000 lbs., featured a new 96-in. "bbc" (bumper-to-back-of-cab) design that combined the cab accessibility of conventional trucks with the payload and maneuverability of the classic cab-over-engine models.

This marked the end of the road for the "cannonballs." The new B-cab conventionals and Tilt-Cabs that came into popular use during the late-1950s and early-1960s also were great chassis for tow trucks, but they lacked that classic sense of nostalgia that the streamlined COEs of the '30s, '40s and early '50s wore so well.

This 1937 GMC COE served a Pontiac dealership in Calumet, Michigan for years. (Terry Patton/ Alan Merkel)

INTERNATIONAL
BRIEF OVERVIEW

By Tom Collins

International began making trucks after more than a half century of success as a farm equipment maker. From 1907 until they were reincorporated as Navistar International in 1986, the International name meant hard-working trucks in models that ranged from small pickups to multiple-ton heavy load carriers. Particularly memorable Internationals are the famed A and C series of the 1930s, the K series of the '40s, the International 6x6 military

trucks and the R series that appeared in the 1950s.

More recent models have included the "star" suffix Internationals that included the Transtar, Loadstar, Paystar, Cargostar and Fleetstar models, among others. Many older Internationals are preserved and treasured. Internationals always have been adapted for many special uses. Today they are found wherever tow vehicles and flatbed carriers are used.

An impressive-looking 1975 International Pay Star served Northbrook Garage, Northbrook, Illinois, in many ways. It is nicknamed "Monster II." (Jay Lorenz)

A 1931 International A series was used by the Rosston Garage of Indiana. Note the chrome rails on the tow body. (OCW)

This International Fleetstar 2070A diesel served Henry's Incorporated of Kaukauna, Wisconsin. (Henry Vanden Heuvel)

Shuler's of Springfield, Ohio, used this International C series, produced between 1934 and 1936. The new truck was photographed in a beautiful park setting. (OCW)

Mike's Auto and Towing of Windsor, Connecticut, uses this 1997 International 4700 with a four-door crew cab and a 22-foot Century flatbed. (Mike Markesich)

JEEP BRIEF OVERVIEW

By Tom Collins

Through various stages of ownership, including Willys-Overland, Kaiser, AMC, and Daimler-Chrysler, the venerable military-based "pack mule" Jeep and its derivatives have become a cultural icon. Jeeps have been popular service and tow vehicles, especially those made in the late 1940s through the 1960s. During World War II, the all-purpose Jeep forever replaced the horse as the ideal infantry vehicle. Willys-Overland brought out the versatile Jeep in civilian form with the CJ series. In 1947, Jeep introduced a 1-ton pickup.

The FC Jeeps, introduced in 1957, offered even more towing appeal. The cab-over-engine 1/2-ton FC 150 rode an 81-in. wheelbase while the 1-ton FC 170 had a 103.5 in. wheelbase. The maneuverable FCs included towing equipment among their available factory options. In 1963, the J series introduced, flared and slab-sided pickups available in 1/2- to 1-ton models and rode in 120- and 126-in. wheelbases.

Through the years, the classic "Army mule" Jeeps became solid citizens back home, especially those used in towing and auto service.

Jeep pickups were versatile vehicles often used by service stations or as part of a tow truck fleet. This one is equipped with a simple but effective tow unit. (OCW)

A 1954 Jeep CJ-5 is prepared for snow and tow! Jeep CJs often were chosen for their versatility, a reputation well earned in World War II. (OCW)

This 1958 Jeep FC 170 worked hard for Henry's of Kaukauna, Wisconsin, an auto body shop that got into the tow business. Jeep FCs brought the engine inside the cab. (Henry Vanden Heuvel)

A MECHANIC'S SPECIAL EDITION JEEP

By Tom Collins

Don Dugal's 1952 Willys Jeep is a special vehicle. You might call it a "mechanic's special." Now housed with a dozen collector vehicles at Don's Woonsocket, Rhode Island, home, this Jeep originally was a utility vehicle for a mobile home park. A practical, low profile Konig utility body was substituted for the standard pickup box early in the Jeep's career. Roll bar protection was added near the rear of the cab.

Over the majority of its life, the Willys Jeep moved motor homes and had just 40,000 miles on its odometer when Don brought it home. It was assembled during the last year Willys produced Jeeps, just prior to Kaiser's purchase of the Toledo, Ohio, based firm.

With more than 60 years experience as a mechanic, Don was confident he could convert the utility Jeep into a tow truck.

One of his first modifications was an engine swap. He replaced the tired original "Hurricane" F head 134-cid 72-hp 4-cylinder engine with a more powerful "Dauntless" 160- hp overhead valve V-6. (Think of comedian Danny Thomas saying "Holy Toledo, what a car!")

Don's idea for a tow boom was to use major sections of a boat trailer. He says it worked well and has decent lifting power for his needs.

Already fitted with a CB radio, police scanner, 8-track player and an array of work lights, Don also added custom orange coach lamps on the front cowl. He repainted the entire Jeep and affixed a Willys service decal on the doors.

The Jeep, which already had a tow truck-like push bumper, now looks ready to rescue an Aero Willys sedan from danger or to bring a Jeep CJ into the shop.

"It always turns heads at a car show," says Don. "I like different vehicles and this one is unique."

The Jeep is his only vehicle that looks like a tow truck, but Don says his '48 Nash Ambassador can tow this Jeep and several vehicles in his collection. The Nash now has 295,000 miles on its odometer and was ready for a 2003 summer trip to California.

You can't beat a solid Jeep—or Nash—in the care of a veteran mechanic.

This 1952 Willys Jeep spent most of its life serving a mobile home park until Don Dugal of Woonsocket, Rhode Island, brought it home and converted it into a tow truck. (Don Dugal)

MACK
BRIEF OVERVIEW

By Tom Collins

From the days of chain drive on through the present, the "Bulldog" hood ornament has stood for toughness around the world. Many Mack trucks have achieved legendary status, including the early AC series, the rock-ribbed BJ series and the L series of the 1940s. The famed B series of the 1950s still has trucks that are in service.

For example, tower Steven Avella of Highpoint Garage in Union City, New Jersey, says he's put 1.5 million miles on his 1956 Mack B-61T tow truck and that total is climbing as he still drives it daily.

Mack's Thermodyne diesels, later followed by their Maxidyne engines, were efficient and dependable for tow operators. Mack merged with Renault of France in the 1980s, then joined forces with Volvo of Sweden in 1993. Restored Macks bring pride to owners and viewers alike while current models continue to command respect on every highway they travel.

This well-used tow truck has lost its headlights over the years. It's a 1948 Mack EQ owned by Forrest Shaffer of Avonmore, Pennsylvania. (Forrest Shaffer)

The proud crew of Worcester, Massachusetts, Mack poses with their veteran 1940 Mack LJ. The veteran Mack seems to have held up well following years of service. (Mack Truck Historical Archives)

The F.W. Fletcher Garage of Fryburg, Pennsylvania, used this 1950 Mack A20H in its Chrysler, Plymouth and Mack dealerships. It poses near an unidentified bridge. (Mack Truck Historical Archives)

This 1922 AB Mack truck featured chain drive and a partially covered towing apparatus. Note the Mack logo on the door and the large cab-mounted spotlight. (Mack Truck Historical Archives)

THE BIG, BEAUTY-CONTEST-WINNING BRUTE

By Tom Collins

You probably wouldn't put a rugged Mack truck in the same category as Miss Universe or Miss America. But this 1952 Mack LJ tow truck is right up there with the brunette from Texas and the lovely Miss Venezuela in taking beauty contest prizes.

The red and white Mack has won first prize in at least three shows it's entered. That's very good for a truck that began its career when Harry Truman was President.

The prize-winning Mack LJ, a series produced from 1940-'56, could have been an aging wallflower instead of a prize winner. Fortunately, this beast became a beauty.

Owner Phil Morrison of Morrison Towing Service, Sullivan, Indiana, was approached by an estate sale executor in 1972 but really wasn't terribly interested in the used Mack. His modest bid was accepted by the estate and the towing veteran was turned over to him.

Just as some beauty contest winners have had cosmetic surgery, the burly bulldog had some work done as well. We won't talk about Miss Tennessee or the entrant from Sweden, but the Mack's engine and transmission received a good going over. The classic truck and Holmes tow unit were restored. The tow body also received some tucks.

The 220-hp Cummins diesel-powered Mack LJ is paired with a Brownlite four-speed transmission. It has chrome on its wheels, upright exhausts, headlights and trim.

The Morrison Mack has won first place in prestigious tow shows in Chattanooga, Tennessee; Lisle, Illinois, as well as the Ohio Tow Show at Huron. It's right up there with the chestnut-eyed Miss Louisiana or the smiling Miss Ghana in accumulating first prize sashes.

While the rest of the Morrison fleet is busy working for a living towing vehicles in southwestern Indiana, the Mack is pampered for its next appearance.

It's a proven winner, a Mack beauty that turns heads.

Beauty is in the eyes of the beholder and in this case, the 1952 Mack LJ, owned by Phil Morrison, has been a consistent show-stopping winner. (Morrison Towing)

The Mack LJ was purchased from an estate and is powered by a 220-hp Cummins diesel engine. (Morrison Towing)

A Mack B series Thermodyne diesel like this one would be a prized restoration. (Mack Truck Historical Archives)

NASH RARE "RAMBLER" WRECKERS

By John Gunnell

In 1916, Charlie Nash stepped down as the boss of General Motors and used the big bucks he'd made to buy a car company in Wisconsin. The Thomas B. Jeffery Co. had started in 1904 with a car called the Rambler and a truck called the Rambler Delivery wagon.

Throughout the '20s and '30s, Nash made cars under his own name. With the heavy demand for vehicles after World War II, he went back to building vehicles with links to the company's past — Ramblers and trucks. The famous Nash Rambler — remember the "beep-beep" song of the '50s? — was one of the first modern compact cars. The Nash "Haul-Thrift" truck was a somewhat brawnier postwar machine. It was also quite rare.

Between 1947 and 1954, Nash built just 4,998 of these trucks in two very similar models: the 3148 with a 133-inch wheelbase and the 3248 with a 157-inch wheelbase. The Nash trucks had limited-production status stemming from the fact they were made primarily for export to other countries. However, Nash dealerships in the United States could order one of these vehicles for use as a tow truck.

Both Nash truck models were powered by the reliable 234.8-cid overhead valve in-line six-cylinder engine, which produced 104-hp at 3400 rpm. It was attached to a four-speed manual transmission. Drive train options included a five-speed gearbox and a Timken double-reduction hypoid vacuum-shift rear axle that increased the number of forward "gears" to eight. Both trucks had 14,000-pound GVW ratings with the standard axle or 15,500 pounds with the two-speed rear. Eight-ply 7.00 x 20 tires were standard equipment and 10-ply 8.25 x 20s could be ordered at extra cost.

The Nash trucks looked particularly distinctive and

Metzler Sales of Oshkosh, Wisconsin, handled Nash, AMC, Jeep, Rambler and Renault vehicles over the years and probably hauled a few of each home with the Nash tow truck. (John Gunnell)

handsome because the body panels used for the fenders, hood, cab and instrument panel were adapted from Nash's large and beautiful Ambassador passenger car. The trucks' radiator grilles were also simplified versions of the Ambassador's grille. Brown vinyl upholstery was used to make the inside of the cab a little bit fancier than the average truck interior of that era.

Even the small Haul-Thrift truck's wheelbase was a foot longer than that of the Ambassador car and its frame construction was strictly heavy-duty. Leaf springs with auxiliary helper springs were used all around. The front and single-speed rear axles were Timken-Detroit units and large Lockheed brakes supplied stopping power.

The Model 3148 made an excellent tow truck and Nash dealers really enjoyed having the same brand of wrecker as the cars they sold. This allowed them to keep up with Chevrolet, Dodge, Ford and Studebaker dealers in terms of image. And, of course, it was even better when they were called out to tow a competing make of automobile into the shop with their dependable Nash tow truck!

One truck pictured here served Metzler Sales Nash dealership in Oshkosh, Wisconsin for many years. The Metzlers are still in the used-car business, but their rare "Rambler" wrecker has been retired and put on the car-show circuit. The accompanying photos of the truck were snapped at the annual Appleton, Wisconsin, Auto Show. This event is held in mid-July in the city's Pierce Park (named after the Pierce fire and utility truck company, by the way.)

The Nash wrecker's hood, fender aprons, grille surround, cab, doors and utility box sides are finished in refrigerator white. The front and rear fenders, frame, tool boxes and diamond-plate "cat walks" are done in dark blue, making the truck look just like it did years ago. Blue-and-red body lettering identifies the dealership and advertises "General Repair & Wrecker Service" as it did in the good old days. "Our wrecker service is ups and downs" says an old company slogan printed on the box sides above the old-fashioned BE5-1310 phone number. The single-boom hoist is done in dark blue and the tow joy is painted white.

Setting off the front of the wrecker is a mass of bright

metal — three wide lower grille bars, four slightly narrower upper grille bars and stainless steel headlamp doors. A colorful, chrome-bordered Nash emblem sets off the truck's nose. Finishing touches include white wheel spiders, bright diamond-plate running boards and a red flashing beacon light on the roof of the cab.

The Nash "Haul-Thrift" truck borrowed its front end sheet metal from the postwar Nash Ambassador car line. It gave the Nash truck a very classy and classic look. (John Gunnell)

Many of the rare postwar Nash trucks were used by Nash dealers as tow trucks. The towing apparatus on this example looks too nice to use these days. (John Gunnell)

The interiors of the Nash trucks, including those used by dealers for towing, were very car-like. (Tom Collins)

A RAMBLER "WRECKCOLLECTION" : EXTREMELY NICE TRUCKS By Bob Loudon

After World War II, I was working as a truck driver for a company called KAT Corporation. KAT was one of the large automobile shippers that Nash-Kelvinator Corporation used back in that era.

In late 1947 or early 1948, Nash-Kelvinator decided to test the market for truck manufacturing. One day, during that winter, I was standing in a Shell gas station across the street from the Nash experimental department having a Coke and gabbing with some of the other KAT truck drivers. We all had our own rigs and we were naturally interested in any kind of truck.

All at once, a beautiful, dark green 2-ton Nash truck pulled up and parked in front of the gas station's door. None of us had ever seen such a truck before and it was obvious that this was the very first one built. The Nash executive driving it had brought it over to show it to us and to get our reactions.

Not being the bashful type, I was the first one out the door. I proceeded to climb in the dark green truck and sat behind the steering wheel. It was a very cold winter day in Wisconsin, but the famous Nash Weather-Eye heating system was doing its job perfectly. It was nice and warm in the cab.

The truck was truly beautiful for its time. The interior was trimmed out much nicer than other trucks of the period. Everything was done in brown vinyl upholstery including the twin sun visors and the door armrests. It had a complete headliner, unlike many other contemporary trucks.

The Nash executive asked my opinion and I told him I had only one question — where could I get a truck like it?

I learned the Nash trucks were built in two configurations: 1-1/2-ton and 2-ton. The smaller models had 7.50 x 20 inch tires and a four-speed gearbox. The 2-ton trucks had 8.25 x 20 tires, heavier springs with overload springs and two-speed rear ends. The engine used in both types was the great Nash-built 234-cid in-line six. This motor was fitted with overhead valves and had seven main bearings. Ross cam-and-lever steering was used and the trucks drove very, very nicely!

About 4,500 Nash trucks were built from then until production ended in 1954. Approximately 700 of these trucks were made into wreckers. I am fortunate enough to own one of the latter units. My truck is the 1-1/2-ton version.

This Nash has an Ashton wrecker conversion, which was made in Detroit, Michigan. The hoist works via a power take off from the transmission, with all controls being mounted at the left rear corner. It still works very nicely and the tow truck is a lot of fun to drive. With the straight rear end, the useable highway speed is about 50-55 mph. The Nash engine is extremely smooth and quiet for a truck and provides plenty of power when compared to the early postwar competition.

All in all, Nash built extremely nice trucks and those who own them soon find they generate a great deal of interest at old car shows.

Bob Loudon used his 1949 Nash wrecker to stage a period scene. The truck looks like it's ready to tow away a disabled Packard of the same era. (Bob Loudon)

STUDEBAKER WHEN DRIVERS BENT 'EM, "SOUTH BENDERS" DRAGGED THEM IN

By John Gunnell

In the mid-1800s, pioneers crossed our great land in Conestoga wagons made by the Studebaker Brothers of South Bend. Later, when towns and cities sprang up, Studebaker commercial wagons transported the goods that people needed. As the automotive age dawned, the Indiana company began to manufacture cars to carry people . . . and trucks to work for them.

Ambulances and police paddy wagons appear to be the first motorized commercial vehicles marketed by Studebaker, around 1908, in cooperation with the Garford Automobile Company.

In 1911, Studebaker hired German designer Albert S. Mais to develop a 3-ton truck. This model didn't reach production, but a year later the Flanders branch of the company offered the passenger-car-based Model 20 Delivery Car. This light-duty truck, on a 100-inch wheelbase, was rated 1/2-ton capacity and was cheap enough, at $800, but not very sturdy.

By November of 1913, the company announced a 3/4-ton truck would join its line in 1914. For the next half-century, Studebaker turned out some of the finest commercial vehicles money could buy. Many found their way into the hands of hardworking vehicle-recovery industry professionals.

The Model 5 Studebaker truck offered Delivery and Express (pickup) bodies. It used a four-cylinder engine and carried a $1,085 price in 1915. This truck would have been too light and underpowered to use for towing. Commercial

This 1927 Studebaker Dictator had an open-cab body and carried an express box and wrecker unit. It may have been a "yard car" used at the Studebaker factory in South Bend, Indiana. [Applegate and Applegate]

Nu-Way Garage in Quebec City, Quebec, found this 1-ton Studebaker perfect for "Day and Night Service." (Applegate and Applegate)

wrecker bodies hadn't been invented. During 1915, Earnest Holmes developed vehicle-recovery equipment for his own use. He tested his twin-boom tow truck in 1916.

About the time Holmes' first wrecker arrived, Studebaker released the Model 7 powered by a larger 40-hp four. It was available in three versions: the 112-inch wheelbase Delivery, and the Jitney Bus in a 13-inch longer stance shared with the Ton Truck. The 1-ton was available with two factory bodies, an Open Express for $1,200 and a Platform Stake for $1,250. The chassis with cab was perfect for mounting a wrecker.

Marque historian Bill Cannon says, "A substantial number of specialized vehicles were built by other firms on the Studebaker commercial vehicle chassis."

The Studebaker Big Six passenger car caught on for towing use. This model arrived at the New York Auto Show in January 1918. This big, rugged automobile had a 126-inch wheelbase and an in-line six-cylinder engine that produced 60 hp. At $2,000, it was a great bargain that was, as Bill Cannon says, "…equally at home on boulevards or in the backwoods."

In addition to hauling around up to seven passengers at high speeds, auto repair shops soon realized the workhorse Big Six and its 50-hp companion the Standard Six (which came out in 1924) could be used to drag in stranded or damaged cars. By the late-'20s, second-hand Studebakers were being stripped for wrecker conversions.

"Numerous exemplary utility and tow vehicles were built on the rugged Big Six and Standard Six chassis," wrote Cannon in his book Studebaker: The Complete Story.

Beginning in 1926, Studebaker re-entered the commercial vehicle market with a line of buses based on the Big Six. Factory-built delivery trucks reappeared in 1927, powered by the passenger car Standard Six. They were renamed Dictator models during the 1927 production

This one-of-a-kind Studebaker tow truck was used by Automovel Club de Portugal for "pronto socorro," literally, "immediate help." It carries a Weaver wrecking crane. (Applegate and Applegate)

A sturdy Studebaker K15-38 1-1/2-ton tow truck has a 138-inch wheelbase and 6.00-20 tires front and rear. It carried a Holmes wrecker body in its work at Mahanoy City, Pennsylvania. (Applegate and Applegate)

were renamed Dictator models during the 1927 production run. A 1-ton commercial chassis was offered in this line. At least one 1927 open-cab Dictator chassis was fitted with shortened roadster coachwork and an express truck body with a wrecker unit mounted on back. A photo shows this truck parked outside the Studebaker factory—perhaps a "yard car" the automaker used when moving cars around.

During this period, sales of expensive cars were impacted by the Great Depression and Pierce-Arrow, a luxury-car maker from Buffalo, New York, linked up with Studebaker. This association led to the formation of the SPA Truck Corporation, which consolidated the resources of the two firms, plus those of White Motor Company, which built White and Indiana trucks.

SPA Truck Corporation suddenly became a major

player in the commercial vehicle field with a new line of hefty 70-hp S-Series Studebaker trucks evolved from this merger. These included the Model GN-20 3/4-ton Delivery Truck with a 115-inch wheelbase, the GN-30 1-ton Commercial Chassis with a 130-inch wheelbase and the GN-40 2-ton Commercial Chassis with a 146-inch wheelbase. All were well-suited for towing use.

Studebaker fell into receivership during 1930 and had to divest its holdings in Pierce-Arrow and White to raise cash. Studebaker trucks continued to be built, with some 2,500 leaving the factory annually in 1931-1933. A 1-1/2-ton model joined the line and was perfect for vehicle recovery work when properly outfitted.

The trucks continued to use the six-cylinder engine and the more powerful Studebaker President straight eight passenger car chassis was available for tow truck conversions.

Belt tightening during the depths of the Great Depression allowed Studebaker to develop new 1934 T-Series trucks. For towing service operators, both the T-2

Demers Brothers, Worcester, Massachusetts, 1939 Studebaker "Tow Cruiser" carried a Holmes "Road King" twin-boom wrecker unit. (Applegate and Applegate)

William Silva Studebaker of Modesto, California, used this handsome 1937 Studebaker J-15 1-1/2-ton tow truck to help its customers and others. (Applegate and Applegate)

Lambert Co. Ltd., a Holmes Wrecker distributor in Southern California, used this photo to promote the dashing Studebaker truck and its Holmes "Road King" wrecker body. (Applegate and Applegate)

1-1/2-ton standard truck and the T-4 1-3/4-ton standard truck were available in 130-, 141- and 165-inch wheelbase configurations. Also available were the T-6 (2-ton) and T-8 (3-ton) standard trucks with longer wheelbases for heavy-duty applications.

One 1934 Studebaker T-2185 1-1/2-ton tow truck was built with an unusual one-piece, streamlined rear body section. This one-of-a-kind creation was employed by the Automobile Club of Portugal and carried a Weaver wrecking crane. Under the hood was the 205.3-cid Dictator six, which developed 88 maximum hp.

The T-Series was followed by the W-Series, which featured models with catchy names like the W-7 Mogul and the W-8 Big Chief. Both were 3-tonners. The Mogul used a Waukesha BK engine and the Big Chief was powered by a Waukesha 6-110 six-cylinder engine. The Model 2T2 Standard Ace truck remained in the T-Series with Studebaker's six for power.

Streamlined styling was a trend in the late-1930s and Studebaker had some of the best thanks to the talents of Brooks Stevens and Raymond Loewy. The J-Series trucks, introduced in 1937, included a full range of models from a passenger-car-based Coupe Express that probably couldn't tow a Bantam car to a 3-ton cab-forward truck with a Hercules engine that could pull a bus out of a ditch. For light-duty vehicle recovery work, the J-15 1-1/2-ton Standard Truck with the big Studebaker six was a great unit. The J20 2-ton Standard Truck used the Hercules JXB motor.

In this era, it became fashionable for Studebaker dealers to advertise their brand using a tow truck. It suggested brand loyalty, and gave potential buyers the opportunity to see a Studebaker truck in action on a regular basis.

For 1938, the "J" turned to a "K," with the same

offerings. A typical rig of this era was a tow truck operated by Penn Garage of Mahanoy City, Pennsylvania. This sturdy Studebaker is a K15-38 1-1/2-ton truck with a 138-inch wheelbase and 6.00-20 tires front and rear. It carried a Holmes wrecker body. Mounted on the back was a 3-1/2-ton capacity power crane made by Marquette Manufacturing Company of Minneapolis, Minnesota. The body was 94 inches long, 46-1/2 inches wide and 22-1/2 inches deep.

The Dictator line was discontinued because of negative connotations of the name after the rise of Adolf Hitler and Benito Mussolini. The Commander name, which disappeared in 1936 and 1937, was revived for Studebaker's Standard Six. The 1938 six grew to 226.2 cid and 90 hp.

The K-Series remained until 1940 in much the same format, as evidenced by a photograph of the "Tow Cruiser." This was the name given to a 1939 K15-62 (162-inch wheelbase) Studebaker tow truck operated by Demers Bros. Garage of Worcester, Massachusetts. It was used in a safety campaign sponsored by the Worcester Citizens Traffic Safety Committee. The Tow Cruiser carried a Holmes "Road King" twin-boom wrecker unit. The truck's nickname most likely was inspired by the Snow Cruiser, a huge $150,000 vehicle built for Admiral Richard Byrd to use in one of his Antarctic expeditions.

It appears Studebaker used Holmes as its primary supplier of wrecker equipment in this era. Another of the automaker's factory publicity photos shows a gorgeous 1939 tow truck with the power-operated Road King wrecker parked in front of Lambert Company Ltd., the West Coast distributor of Holmes equipment. Lettered on the sides of the truck is the slogan, "The Big Profit Jobs Don't Drive In – They Are Towed In!"

Studebaker's last prewar trucks, the M-Series, were comprised of smaller trucks employing the Champion six-cylinder engine and heavy-duty models with the

Because Studebakers were built in the Hoosier State—Indiana—it was common to see them used at the Indianapolis Motor Speedway. This is a 1959 Transtar V-8 with a Holmes 400 RW wrecker unit. (Applegate and Applegate)

Commander Six under their hoods. There also was an L-series Coupe Express, but it was based on passenger-car running gear. Some of the M-Series trucks were produced in military versions for World War II. The M-Series joined all prewar models in production just after the war ended. A new model was the 2-on M17, for export only. These trucks had a tall center grille section flanked by lower grilles across the fender catwalks on each side.

Famed Studebaker designer, Robert Bourke, was responsible for the postwar R-Series that debuted in 1949. The 2R10 3/4-ton trucks were best-suited for light-duty use and employed a 170-cid 80-hp six. The 2R17 2-ton models with a 226-cid 94-hp six were better suited for vehicle recovery work. In the early '50s, the smaller engine was upped to 85 hp while a 245-cid 100-102 hp engine became the Big Six. In 1953, Barksdale Motors, Inc., a Studebaker dealer in Bossier City, Louisiana, operated a heavy-duty wrecker built on a 1-1/2-ton R-Series Studebaker chassis-cab with the larger engine. In 1954, the 3R models with one-piece windshields replaced the split-windshield 2R versions.

In 1955, the handsome R-Series evolved into the E-Series which used a range of different engines including a 185-cid six with 92 hp, the 102 hp 225-cid six, a 224-cid V-8 with 140 hp or a 156 hp 259-cid V-8. Both V-8s could be fitted with an optional four-barrel carburetor that gave them approximately 20 additional horsepower. The E-Series had a larger rear window and the grille featured three vertical members that divided the opening into four "boxes" between the single headlights.

With the optional V-8s, the heavier-duty E-Series Studebakers made great tow trucks. Because Studebakers were built in Indiana, it was common to see them used at the Indianapolis Motor Speedway in the '50s and early '60s.

Also available in 1960 were the light-duty Champ models. They shared their front-end sheet metal with the new Lark passenger car and came in 1/2- and 3/4-ton models. These were of some interest for use in neighborhood service stations and garages. It was possible to get a Champ set up as a wrecker.

Studebaker trucks generally were unchanged from 1961 through the end of truck production in 1964. New diesel engines were made available in the 1-1/2-, 2-ton and heavy-duty 2-ton 7E-series Transtars in 1962. They used four-cylinder Detroit Diesel engines made by General Motors and did yeoman work for vehicle-recovery professionals. A three-cylinder 3-53 GM diesel engine was added in 1963 for 1- and 1-1/2-ton trucks.

Unfortunately, sales of less than 10,000 units per year added little to Studebaker's coffers and the company's car and truck business was sinking fast by the early '60s. Truck production virtually doubled in 1963, due to a one-time government order for Postal Vans. After that, it was slow going again. On December 27, 1963 Studebaker Corporation built its last civilian truck. The history of Studebaker trucks — and Studebaker tow trucks — had come to its end.

In 1953, Barksdale Motors, Inc., the Studebaker dealer in Bossier City, Louisiana, operated a heavy-duty wrecker built on a 1-1/2-ton R-Series Studebaker chassis-cab and powered by a Big Six engine. (Applegate and Applegate)

WHITE
BRIEF OVERVIEW

By Tom Collins

Now part of the White/ Volvo Corporation, White trucks began to roll across American roads and streets in 1901 when Rollin, Walter and Windsor White began building their dependable machines in Cleveland, Ohio. White trucks served in almost every conceivable manner and worked in dozens of professions, carrying loads that ranged from aardvarks to watermelons and everything in between.

In the 1930s, when streamlining influenced automotive design, White employed flamboyant Russian-born Count Alexis de Sakhnoffsky to create their stunning 700 series streamlined cab over engine which debuted in 1936.

The classic tractor-trailer combination built for Labatt Breweries of London, Ontario, represent the best of White streamlining. Labatt also employed an equally stylish tow truck of the same genre.

Also famous was their long-running W and WC series, and the later 3000 and 4000 series. White produced two durable truck lines with Freightliner, which originated in Salt Lake City, Utah, and with Canadian-born Western Star. The company now is part of White/ Volvo. White trucks represent a vital portion of North American commerce, including the towing industry.

The Gilder Brothers of North Ridgeville, Ohio, used this 1948 WA-22 White tow truck in their towing business. (Bob Gilder)

Mike's Auto and Towing of Windsor, Connecticut, uses this 1987 Western Star with its 45-ton Attac tow crane. (Mike Markesich)

The 1971 White Western Star carries a Holmes 750 tow unit and is powered by a 335 cid Cummins diesel. It's used every day at Middleton Towing, Engadine, Michigan. (Ron Kowalke)

The fleet of Bill's Service, Windsor, Connecticut included a 1964 White 9000 along with a 1972 Chevrolet C-30 and a '90 C-60 Chevy—all Holmes equipped. (Mike Markesich)

WHITE STREAMLINED WHITE TOW TRUCKS ARE "OBJETS D'ART"

By Tom Collins

One of the prolific designers in the automotive world of the 1930s was Count Alexis de Sakhnoffsky, a refugee from the Bolshevik Revolution who learned automotive engineering after emigrating to Switzerland.

De Sakhnoffsky was heavily involved in the streamlined look of cars in the 1930s and worked on designs for Cord, Nash and the Chrysler Airflow. In 1935, the White Motor Company of Cleveland, Ohio, and its Canadian subsidiary, asked him to help with a project for John Labatt Breweries, Limited, of London, Ontario.

Labatt wanted to promote its beer throughout Canada with a distinctive looking delivery truck and trailer combination.

De Sakhnoffsky designed the winning look which appeared in its first series in 1936. A flowing White tractor cab complimented the streamlined trailer, originally built by the Fruehauf Corporation. Two more truck series were produced for Labatt, one of which won a 1939 design award.

Not as well known as the beer hauling Labatt Whites are their sculptured White tow trucks. White conventional cabs were accented with chromed wheel trim rings, lug nuts, dual front bumpers, headlight rims, spotlights, dual horns and even turn signals.

The radiators and folding hood sported double layers of chrome accents flowing back toward the cowl. Chrome accents were repeated on the highly streamlined tow body. and accents that matched the cab. One version also

One of the early Labatt Brewery delivery trucks has been restored. It was a trend-setting exercise in design and function. (OCW)

included stylish wheel covers.

The running lights and windshield wiper housings were streamlined on some models. The Labatt logo was painted over the windshield, on cab doors and tow body and was chromed in large letters on the radiator on some Labatt tow trucks.

Reportedly, a Labatt White streamlined beer truck has been restored in Canada. It would be interesting to learn if one of these striking tow trucks has survived.

It's a tow truck work of art.

This Labatt Brewery tow truck is equipped with a front winch. Its plaque proclaims the allegiance of brewery workers, delivery drivers and body makers. (Labatt Brewery)

In addition to the beautiful Alexis de Sahknoffsky-designed beer delivery trucks by White, the Labatt Brewery of London, Ontario, used equally stylish tow trucks. (Labatt Brewery)

MISCELLANEOUS HAUL OF FAME NORTH AMERICA

Everyone recognizes the most common names in U.S. trucks: Chevrolet, Ford, Dodge and GMC. Here are other existing American manufacturers who have made, or still make, tow truck chassis in the United States. We've done our best not to ignore anyone.

FWD (FWD/Seagrave)	1909-present	Clintonville, Wisconsin
Hendrickson	1913-present	Chicago, Illinois
International (I-H/ Navistar)	1907-present	Chicago, Illinois
Jeep (Daimler-Chrysler)	1941--present	Toledo, Ohio
Kenworth	1923-present	Seattle, Washington
Mack	1902-present	Allentown, Pennsylvania
Oshkosh	1917-present	Oshkosh, Wisconsin
Peterbuilt	1939-present	Oakland/Newark, California
Walter	1909-present	Voorheesville, New York
White (White/ Volvo)	1901-present	Cleveland, Ohio

No "Haul" of Fame would be complete without these past American tow truck makers:

Autocar	1897-1995	Ardmore, Pennsylvania
Biederman	1920-1955	Cincinnati, Ohio
Brockway	1912-1977	Cortland, New York
Corbitt	1913-1958	Henderson, North Carolina
Diamond T	1911-1966	Chicago, Illinois
Fageol	1916-1954	Oakland, California
Federal	1910-1959	Detroit, Michigan
Garford	1909-1933	Lima, Ohio
Graham Brothers	1919-1928	Detroit, Michigan / Evansville, Indiana
Hug	1922-1942	Highland, Illinois
Indiana	1911-1939	Marion, Indiana/ Cleveland, Ohio
Kissel	1908-1931	Hartford, Wisconsin
Nash	1947-1955 (export)	Kenosha, Wisconsin
Packard	1905-1923	Detroit, Michigan
Pierce Arrow	1910-1932	Buffalo, New York
REO	1908-1967	Lansing, Michigan
Schacht	1910-1938	Cincinnati, Ohio
Studebaker	1902-1964	So. Bend, Indiana
Velie	1911-1929	Moline, Illinois
Ward La France	1919-1993	Elmira, New York

The monogrammed "G" identifies this Guaranteed Motor Towing Service 1972 Oshkosh. It began life hauling concrete mix in Florida. (Mark Redman)

White's of Waltham, Massachusetts, used this 1977 Brockway 761 heavy duty tow truck. It features a fiberglass tilt nose. (OCW)

HAUL OF FAME INTERNATIONAL

Here is a partial list of truck makers past and present from around the world. Many make tow truck chassis or have had their trucks converted to tow vehicles:

Alfa Romeo (Italy)	Atkinson (U.K.)	Austin (U.K.)
Bedford (U.K.)	Berliet (France)	Berna (Switzerland)
Citroen (France)	Commer (U.K.)	DAF (Holland)
Datsun (Japan)	Dennis (U.K.)	Dennison (Ireland)
ERF (U.K.)	FAUN (Germany)	Fiat (Italy)
Foden (U.K.)	GAZ (Russia)	Gotfredson (Canada)
Hayes (Canada)	Hino (Japan)	Isuzu (Japan)
Isotta-Fraschini (Italy)	Jae Fong (China)	Jelcz (Poland)
Karrier (U.K.)	Krupp (Germany)	Latil (France)
Leyland (U.K.)	Magirus-Deutz (Germany)	MAN (Germany)
Maudslay (U.K.)	MAZ (Russia)	Mazda (Japan)
Mercedes Benz (Germany)	Merryweather (U.K.)	Miesse (Belgium)
Mitsubishi (Japan)	Morris (U.K.)	Nissan (Japan)
Opel (Germany)	Panhard (France)	Pegaso (Spain)
Peugeot (France)	Praga (Czech Republic)	Raba (Hungary)
Renault (France)	Rover (U.K.)	Saurer (Switzerland)
Saviem (France)	Scammell (U.K.)	Scania (Sweden)
Seddon (U.K.)	SISU (Finland)	Skoda (Czech Rep.)
SR (Rumania)	STAR (Poland)	Steyr (Austria)
TAM (Yugoslavia)	Tatra (Czech Republic)	Terberg (Holland)
Thornycroft (U.K.)	Toyota (Japan)	UNIC (France)
URAL (Russia)	Volvo (Sweden)	Vulcan (U.K.)
Walter (Czechoslovakia)	Willeme (France)	Yue Loong (Taiwan)
ZIL (Russia)	ZIS (Russia)	

A 1945 Reo tow truck appears to be a military veteran that was repainted for civilian use. Note the dual tow body lights and engine mounted vertical exhaust stack. (OCW)

Ken Havekost of Monroe, Michigan, restored a 1949 Nash wrecker and labeled it "Ken's Nash Motors." These Nash car-bodied trucks draw lots of attention at car shows today. (OCW)

A Canadian-built Scot tow truck works in New Hampshire for Mel's Truck Sales of North Hampton, New Hampshire. That's a Holmes mount the Scot is carrying. (Mark Redman)

A Dodge tow truck is a rolling advertisement for this Dodge dealership. (OCW)

The Beach Boys sang about their "409" but they probably never imagined a Chevy-powered 409-cid V-8 in a tow truck used by Hap Cramer in the early '60s. (Hap Cramer)

This 1959 Mack B-8136 6 x 6 was made in Canada. It was spotted at an American Truck Historical Society show at Syracuse, New York. (Mark Redman)

Schamberger Motors used this 1953 Chevrolet at their Nash and Rambler dealership. It has a light duty tow boom and large push bumper. (John Gunnell)

Bob Loudon's 1949 Nash tow truck was available only to Nash dealers in North America. Using car parts made it a very graceful looking tow truck. (Bob Loudon)

CHAPTER 3
TOW MAKERS

HOLMES 485 THE ULTIMATE IN WRECKING EQUIPMENT

By John Gunnell

The Ernest Holmes Company, of Chattanooga, Tenn., is a well-known maker of wrecker bodies for trucks. In 1930, the Holmes 485 was promoted as "The Ultimate in Wrecking Equipment." Its manufacturer claimed that the 485 would allow one man to handle 99 out of every 100 automobile recovery jobs.

The 485 wrecker unit was designed to fit a small truck, but its double swinging booms gave it big capabilities in the field. In addition to the booms, it consisted of a framework made up of tubular steel members and a hoisting mechanism equipped with two speeds and a full-floating power shaft.

The framework was mounted on a heavy steel bolster, reinforced and cushioned with large hickory sill filling the entire channel. The upright masts, booms and brace legs

were made of extra-heavy tubing, while all castings or fittings, except the drums and sheave wheels, were made of forged steel or malleable iron.

Ample size clamp fittings were fitted to the masts and had small projections that engaged holes drilled in the masts to prevent them from slipping or turning. The upper cross member of the frame was heavy steel channel. It had two electric light sockets fitted for illumination of nighttime tow work by contemporary automobile headlight globes. Armored cables and metal covers were provided to protect the electric wiring for the lights.

The hoisting mechanism was designed to carry the service drum on a hollow shaft, through which the low-speed power shaft passed. The power shaft turned on bronze bushings that kept it free of any load. The mechanism

The illustration shows how a tow operator could comfortably operate a Holmes 485 to haul a wrecked touring car from a roadside ditch. (Bob Pierce)

incorporated brass gears providing a high-gear ratio of 4.5:1 and a low-gear ratio of 21:1.

This gave towing leverage of 13.5:1 and 63:1, respectively, using a single line. The leverages were doubled when using block in line.

According to Holmes, the two-speed hoisting mechanism gave the operator of the 485 a service line pull equal to the power exerted by 42 men. Combined with the extreme height of the double booms, the power gave a single tow truck driver the ability to lift, right, secure and tow practically every wrecked vehicle in an easy and efficient manner.

The full-floating hollow drum shaft made hoisting 50 percent easier by entirely eliminating any line-pull braking effect on the drum. The hoisting mechanism was 42 inches from the ground and in easy reach of the operator. In addition to the hoisting mechanism, each derrick was provided with a hoisting drum to regulate the height of the boom.

The lower end of each mast used in the Holmes 485 was fitted with outrigger legs (jacks) made of high-grade iron. These could be lowered automatically by a slight pull on a spring plunger. A large steel pin was placed in the upper exposed hole below the end of the mast. The pin took the derrick's load and transferred it directly to the road, so a small vehicle fitted with a "485" could pull a much larger vehicle out of a jam.

Each derrick was fitted with 7-foot, 8-in. long independent booms and 100 feet of service line. The booms were supported and adjusted by 3/8-inch "cast steel" flexible cables running through suitable cable guides. They could be locked together for towing purposes.

There were provisions for mounting a high-speed 6-volt motor that, with proper gear reduction, gave 492:1 leverage over a load. The electric motor did not interfere with hand operation of the mechanism.

The two derricks could be operated separately or combined as a single unit. Each was supplied with a separate hoisting mechanism. The height of the double adjustable booms allowed the tow truck to remain parallel to the road while recovering a wreck, alleviating traffic blockage.

Pulling power of the Holmes 485 was rated at 2 tons when a single line was being used. That doubled to 4 tons when the end of the line was brought back and anchored to a fixed object and service line blocking was used. Equipment furnished with the wrecker unit included two operating cranks, one service line block and one pair of standard Holmes V tow bars.

The Holmes 485 was only 5 ft. 6 in. overall length and 6 ft. 5 in. wide. The length and width of the body were 5 ft. by 3 ft. 4 in (40 in.) The height over the car or truck frame was 6 ft. The unit weighed only 1,100 lbs. complete and the shipping weight was 228 lbs. heavier.

The No. 485 Holmes Automobile Wrecker unit was built by Holmes in its Chattanooga, Tennessee, factory. The unit was designed to fit on small trucks like this roadster pickup or converted passenger cars. (Bob Pierce)

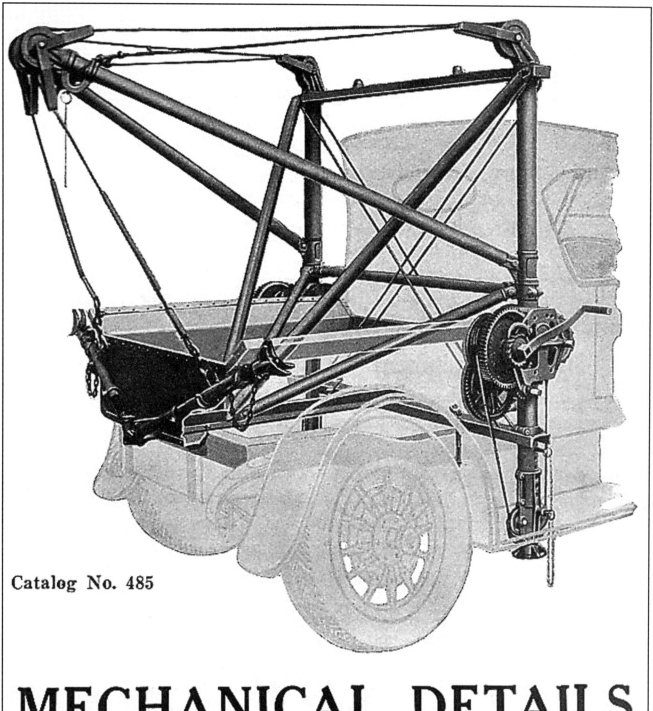

Catalog No. 485

MECHANICAL DETAILS

Mechanical details of the Holmes 485 combined to make it an attractive-looking and powerful device. (Bob Pierce)

THE TOW KING OF NEW YORK

By John Gunnell

Al Barcelow started his "million dollar dream" with a minimal cash investment, but maximum support from a well-known wrecker manufacturer and his banker in Buffalo, New York. His company – Al's Enterprises – was founded on January 1, 1970. By the time he ceased being a distributor for the Ernest C. Holmes Co., in December 1988, Barcelow had gained notoriety as "The Tow King of N.Y."

Al, who celebrated his 79th birthday in January 2004, says he made a lot of friends while running his Holmes distributorship. "When you sold a tow truck to somebody, they made money with it and you made a friend for life," he explains. Al was so good at making new friends that he had the top distributorship in the state of New York and

Al's Enterprises was the place to go for Holmes towing equipment in the greater Buffalo, New York, area. (Al Barcelow)

Al Barcelow was known as the "Tow King of New York" in the 1970s. (Al Barcelow)

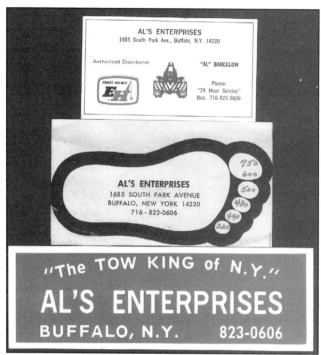

A look at some of the business cards of the "Tow King," Al Barcelow. Now retired in California, Al enjoys collecting and showing license plates. (Al Barcelow)

won sales prizes like a new Chevrolet and a trip to Paris, France.

Things began with much less fanfare. Barcelow started with a single cab-and-chassis truck that he purchased from a local car dealer in Buffalo. He then drove the incomplete truck 850 miles to the Ernest C. Holmes Co. plant in Chattanooga, Tennessee. There, he had one of their wrecker bodies mounted on the chassis and the completed truck was painted. As Barcelow recalls, "In 1970, you could buy a Holmes wrecker unit with all the bells and whistles on it for $6,900."

After Holmes personnel assembled the tow truck, Al drove it back to Buffalo and called on service stations and body shops until the truck was sold. He recalls there were a lot of "mom and pop" gas stations back then that needed tow trucks to keep up with the competition. Once a truck was sold, Barcelow would start the whole process over again.

Each time he headed south, Al set up a schedule with Holmes. The company would give him an appointment to install the tow truck conversion on a designated day.

"You usually got there the day before and they'd give you passes to Lookout Mountain or one of the other local attractions," he remembers. "I was selling so many rigs, I got to know the Chattanooga area pretty well."

Before long, Al found himself hiring a second driver and taking two tow trucks to Tennessee at one time. Then he got up to four trucks.

"Finally, the 1,700-mile round trips got to be a drag," Barcelow relates. "I figured that I could buy wrecker units from Holmes, have them sent to Buffalo and hire a crew to assemble them at home."

In 1972, with his local bank's cooperation, Al purchased a 10-bay building on South Park Avenue (Route 62). That's where he did his own wrecker installations and painting for the next 16 years.

Al hired Ken Burch to work for him as shop manager and keep the business running smoothly. He continued buying chassis-and-cab trucks from local commercial vehicle dealers. Holmes shipped the wrecker units and equipment to Al's Enterprises.

His employees did all of the final assembly and paintwork. In the meantime, Al would put some demo trucks together in different colors and start making his rounds in Western New York.

Barcelow became an associate member of the Greater Buffalo Autobody Guild and the organization featured Al's Enterprises in a 1976 edition of its newsletter.

"The business has risen from that first tow truck sale to sales of close to one half million (dollars), with 'Al' doing all the selling himself," wrote Bill Gallant. "He feels (that) a closely run organization is better controlled and he can stay 'right on top of everything.'" In the story, Al credited his success to "the cooperative response he receives from all the fine people at the Holmes plant in Tennessee, along with his local banking people who placed trust in him."

During 1976, things were going so well that Barcelow purchased a new parts truck, which he painted red, white and blue in honor of the United States Bicentennial. He told Bill Gallant that he really enjoyed his Holmes distributorship and had found the tow truck business to be his "calling in life." At that time Barcelow predicted that, if the Good Lord was willing, he'd retire within the next 10 years, after achieving his "million dollar dream."

Barcelow vividly recalls 1977 as "the year of the big blizzard." He'll never forget one call to a location that was normally a 20-minute drive away. It took him from 10 a.m. to 5 p.m. in the worst storm of the year.

"If I hadn't been in a tow truck, I would not have made it back," he believes. But the extremely heavy snow actually

The Holmes-equipped Buffalo, New York, Fire Department Mack is in action at an accident scene. (Richard Sikora)

aided his business. "I sold every truck I had and every set of tire chains," laughs Al. "We just cleared house at that time."

By the 1980s, Barcelow started seeing big changes in the industry, some good and some not so good.

"We started with mechanical, chain-driven wreckers, then went into hydraulics and then started handling tilt-bed trucks as well. For awhile, when they first came out, I became a distributor of Jerr-Dan tilts, but I went back to Holmes when they started making them," Al advises.

He estimates that during the '70s and '80s, the price of the basic chassis-and-cab truck went up about $500 per year, as did the price of the "back end" of a tow truck.

"Today the cost of an entry-level 1-ton wrecker is a minimum of $50,000," he says. "That's why corner gas stations can't buy them today. For me, 1988 was the right time to get out of the business and I'm glad that I hit it right."

This Mack tow truck, equipped with a Holmes 1701 unit, was used for many years by the Buffalo, New York, Fire Department. (Richard Siko)

THE WRECKER WITH AN ANCHOR: HUBBARD

By John Gunnell

A new feature at the Indiana Towing and Wrecker Association's trade show in 2002 was the first annual "Vintage Show Featuring Hubbard Equipment." The ITWA organized classes for the oldest Hubbard tow truck, the most unique Hubbard, the Hubbard driven farthest to the show and the most beautiful Hubbard. The awards were created to show that the Hoosier State tow men had pride for the equipment made by a company from their home state.

The Hubbard Garage and Repair Center started before World War I in the town of Farmland, Indiana. The company entered the tow truck manufacturing industry in 1922. It was still around until very recently.

According to *The World History of the Towing & Recovery Industry*, Hubbard's business "grew from servicing the many needs of the automobile industry, to creating a means of transporting disabled vehicles, to manufacturing heavy-duty wreckers with maximum lift capability through innovative H-frame design and patented stiff-leg capability."

The company was founded by garage man Oscar Hubbard, who had taken engineering and drafting courses through correspondence schools. Oscar was fascinated with the Weaver Auto Crane that was developed in nearby Illinois.

In 1922, he designed his own vehicle recovery unit, which he exhibited at the Indiana State Fair.

Within a few years, advertisements for a Hubbard power-driven crane were appearing in early automotive trade journals such as *Motor*. The A-frame type crane was designed to fit the frames of big classic cars like Lincolns and Cadillacs. The motor that powered the crane also ran an air pump used for on-the-road tire repairs.

Later, Hubbard became famous for a heavy-duty wrecker design that featured an H-shaped frame on its rear deck. This allowed the boom to be set at different heights and provided extra lifting capacity. A hydraulically-operated spade near the tailboard of the tow vehicle could be raised or lowered to provide "stiff-leg" support.

Around 1940, Hubbard produced an early type of underlift device that some experts believe was the first of its type used in the vehicle-recovery industry. Hubbard power wreckers were often seen on Chevrolet trucks. The Hubbard company was an "approved" supplier listed in the Silver Book, an annual guide to factory-recommended vocational equipment for Chevrolet trucks.

Oscar Hubbard lived until 1953. Son, John, and his son-in-law, Don Wagner, ran the company for 32 years after Oscar's death. In 1985, it was purchased by Jim Ramey.

Philip Hubbard of Onsted, Mich., no relation to the Indiana Hubbards, has a great love of Hubbard tow trucks. In 1985, just before the company was sold to Jim Ramey, Phillip saw an advertisement for a Hubbard wrecker in the 1946 edition of the *Chevrolet Silver Book*. Struck by the name similarity, he had to make a trip to from his home in eastern Michigan to the small Indiana town, near Muncie, where the wreckers bearing his surname were made.

"I learned that Hubbard Mfg. Co. had been making wreckers since 1925," says Phillip. "The Hubbard family was still making wreckers and even helped me find one – a 1946 Chevrolet. This was the first wrecker built on a Chevrolet chassis following World War II. Being an early 1946 model with a painted grille, Oscar Hubbard changed it to a chrome one."

According to Phil Hubbard, his truck didn't come with a spare tire, because rubber was still in short supply right after WWII. When Hubbard mounted the wrecker equipment to his truck, the spare tire carriers were discarded.

His truck also has 1938 Chevrolet rear fenders, which Hubbard used until their inventory was gone. Though not huge like some of today's massive tow trucks, Phil's Chevrolet has a Hubbard-powered winch with a 20-ton capacity. Built-in side compartments are provided for tool and towing equipment storage.

Phil Hubbard's business – Hubbard Auto Center – also owns a second 1946 Hubbard wrecker. Ironically, the black 1-1/2-ton Chevy has prewar styling while the white 1-ton version has postwar styling, though both were titled as 1946 models.

The prewar design was carried over after the war, then changed in the middle of the 1946 model year, when postwar-styled 1947 trucks were just entering production.

(Thanks to Phillip Hubbard for the information and photos.)

This Hubbard-bodied 1-1/2-ton 1946 Chevrolet carries the prewar styling that was used just after WWII. Owner Phillip Hubbard has dressed up the Chevy with chrome and whitewalls. He's no relation to the tow truck builders. (Phillip Hubbard)

Phillip Hubbard of Onsted, Michigan, owns a later series 1946 Chevrolet 1-ton wrecker with Hubbard-built apparatus. This Chevy is white with blue tow crane artfully striped in white. (Phillip Hubbard)

WELD BUILT'S AIM WAS TO DO IT RIGHT!

By John Gunnell

The right model wrecker for the right job at the right price." Weld Built Body Co., Inc., used that motto back in "the good old days." Perhaps that's why Weld Built is, currently, among the oldest towing equipment manufacturing firms in the United States.

According to General Manager Harry E. Brown, Weld Built has been in business since 1948. Today the firm operates on a four-acre site approximately 30 miles from New York City and manufactures over 30 different mechanical and hydraulic wreckers ranging in capacity from 3-ton to 40-ton models. The company's customers include professional tow men, collision shops, automobile clubs, utility companies, the U.S. Military, national fleet accounts, various local municipalities (including New York City) and

This style of Advance-Design Chevrolet truck was built from 1947 to early 1955. Only the 1954 and early '55 models used this cross-bar grille. (John Lee)

overseas markets.

Socrates Katsiamides, of East Stroudsburg, Pennsylvania, can't help thinking that the Wyandanch, New York, based tow-truck-building company had the right idea back in the '50s. He feels Weld Built manufactured some of its best products in that era. That's why Katsiamides decided to restore a 1954 Chevrolet Weld Built wrecker about three years ago.

For many years, Weld Built Body Co. had been located at 5903 Preston Court, in Brooklyn, New York. The company became an "approved" supplier of vocational equipment — such as winches, plows and wrecker bodies — for Chevrolet trucks. Each year, its products were featured in a publication known as the *Silver Book* that commercial vehicle buyers used to help them select special bodies and equipment for their new trucks.

In 1954, if a tow truck operator became interested in purchasing a new Advance-Design Chevrolet truck, he or she could visit the local Chevrolet dealership to purchase a chassis-and-cab unit. The salesperson — who more than likely specialized in commercial sales — would refer to the *Silver Book* to pick the various products that companies like Weld Built could supply.

Weld Built wreckers were nationally known for being strong and power-packed. Collins Associates, Inc., of Cincinnati, Ohio, served as national distributors for Weld Built Body Co. and provided catalogs and other sales literature that promoted the company's products.

Factory literature of the day said that Weld Built models were "built of tested, sure-service materials" and boasted that they were "engineered and constructed to do a fast, dependable job, no matter how tough." In addition to wrecker bodies, Weld Built sold a very complete line of equipment that could handle any towing job from small to big.

"Only Weld Built power wreckers offers you so much for so little!" said one of the firm's *Silver Book* advertisements. Another claimed that "15 needed items comprise America's most complete line with any type needed for any purpose." The line included six models of double booms in 8- to 40-ton capacities, five models of single booms in 4- to 15-ton capacities and four models of drag line trunches. Available accessories included a 6.78-foot snow plow unit with a combination front push plate. In addition, the tower could order six models of wheel dollies, joy bars and tow hitches or a patented telescoping tow bar.

Socrates Katsiamides' truck carries a Weld Built mechanical wrecker boom and body that was available from the late 1940s through the early 1950s. That means it likely is the original body mounted on this particular truck, even though Katsiamides purchased the vehicle used. The boom utilizes a single 12,000-pound winch powered by a clutch-operated power-take-off mechanism.

According to Weld-Built's Harry E. Brown, the manual telescoping boom extension on the truck is of a type used exclusively for engine hoisting. According to Harry E. Brown, "This workhorse was affectionately called the 'banana boom' because of its unique design." Apparently, the original owner of this truck had engine repair jobs in mind, as well as towing work.

Socrates Katsiamides already had four tow trucks working at his general auto repair business, in East Stroudsburg, when he purchased his 1954 Chevrolet 4100 Series Weld Built wrecker in 1971. The truck had previously been owned by a Shell gas station owner who operated on Astoria Boulevard, at 49th Street, in Queens, New York.

"I drove the truck from New York City to Pennsylvania," Katsiamides recalled. By that time, the tow truck was 17 years old and in need of some equipment repairs. Socrates noticed that it was fitted with a Weld Built body and looked the firm up. He found that Weld Built Body Co., Inc., had moved from Brooklyn. It was listed as a Long Island business at that time. Since Katsiamides had to have new cables installed, the truck traveled to Long Island to get the work completed.

"It was old even back then and I used it only on special occasions, for many years, before I decided to restore it in 2000," says Katsiamides, who is now retired from the garage business, but still working. He owns the 209 Diner on Route 209 in East Stroudsburg.

Katsiamides' Advance-Design Chevrolet truck is still powered by its original 235-cid overhead-valve, in-line six-cylinder engine. The electrical wiring package, originally a 6-volt system, has been converted to 12 volts. The truck is refinished in a reddish-orange color with white contrasting paint on the hood, roof, upper cab and upper section of the wrecker body. The winch, operated by means of a power-take-off unit, is still totally functional.

Today, Weld Built Body Company has a 49-person corporate staff handling $3 to $4 million in equipment sales annually. In addition, a network of salespeople cover both local transactions and sales outside the New York Metropolitan area.

According to Harry E. Brown, "Weld Built maintains an excellent reputation for quality towing equipment and superior service propagated by decades of dedication to the towing industry.

Information and photos of Socrates Katsiamides' truck supplied by John Lee; company information supplied by Harry E. Brown.

Weld Built Body Co
276 Long Island Ave
Wyandanch, NY 11798
Phone: 516-643-9700
Fax: 516-491-4728

Weld Built's graceful curved tow boom featured a PTO that drove the winch. (John Lee)

TOW EQUIPMENT SUPPLIES PAVED THE WAY *By Tom Collins*

Just as early trucks were made by dozens of manufacturers, so was early towing equipment. Names like Reliable of Ashland, Ohio; Manley from York, Pennsylvania or the distinctly curved Marquette crane from Minneapolis, Minnesota, once were commonly used. Many small manufacturers also produced tow equipment.

The back cover of the 1924 Chilton Automobile Directory shows an ad for the Manley Wrecking Crane, among other products. (John Gunnell)

One early tow and auto repair equipment leader was Weaver Manufacturing of Springfield, Illinois. It also had operations in Chatham, Ontario and Bedford, England.

The famous Weaver Auto Crane Model G was a hand-cranked unit housed in a compact frame. It was easily mounted in small pickup boxes or converted touring sedans of the 1920s. The crane unit extended over the back end of the tow vehicle and could easily be raised or lowered in a three-foot arc.

Weaver also produced what were called "auto" and "truck ambulances." These two-wheeled, "U"-shaped cradles could be positioned under front or rear axles of cars and trucks to easily tow or move various sized cars and trucks.

The Weaver Towing Pole was an adjustable iron rod with clamps on either end and a spring attached about 2/3 of the way along. Easily connectable to bumpers, springs or axles, it allowed tow operators to push or pull a vehicle and to turn corners. The pole prevented the towed vehicle from swinging into the tow vehicle on a hill or in traffic.

At one time, Weaver was the world's largest auto repair equipment manufacturer. They also produced a 2 hp engine for the Weaver Power Wrecking Crane that could lift 3 ? tons. It was very adequate for most 1920s era tow shops. The unit included conveniently mounted gear shift, clutch and brake levers.

In the 1920s, the Springfield, Illinois, manufacturer advertised that every "complete" towing service needed this combination: a crane, auto ambulance, towing pole and safety service can—all crafted by Weaver.

The Weaver name now survives in memory only, but at one time it was one of the leading tow equipment makers and helped advance the towing industry.

CHAPTER 4
TOUGH TRUCKS

MILITARY MONSTERS

By John Gunnell

The development of a mechanized army unfolded slowly. The "army mule" had long been considered an icon and soldiers — like other Americans — were aware of a growing competition between machine and beast. At the turn of the century and for a few years afterwards, military commanders resisted adoption of the smokey, smelly horseless carriages.

Around 1900 some Woods electrics were sent to the Philippines for use by U. S. occupation forces, but there's no indication that motor cars had been employed stateside by then. It wasn't until 1912, in an army trial from Washington D.C. to Ft. Benjamin Harrison, near Indianapolis, Indiana, that serious testing of trucks for military use was done. Seven trucks started the 1,500-mile trip, but only two finished. It took them 45 days.

In 1915, the army owned just 80 trucks and 35 automobiles. Then Gen. Pershing took a fleet of Dodges, among other vehicles, to Mexico to chase down Pancho Villa and things began to change. Soon after entering World War I, the government purchased 10,550 trucks and 500 motorcycles and the "war on wheels' was underway.

It didn't take long to realize fighting vehicles could break, whether from hard use or incoming artillery shells. A photo in Fred W. Crismon's book U.S. Military Vehicles shows a 1918 Velie truck with a primitive wrecker body at Kelly Field in Texas. It may be the first documented military recovery vehicle — but it wasn't the last.

By 1920, huge wreckers were hauling large army trucks out of trouble. Crismon's book shows a Liberty truck fitted with twin-boom wrecking equipment winching a similar truck to safety.

"This wrecker mechanism was considered innovative in

Dressed in its "military fatigues" is this Connecticut Army National Guard 1991 AM General M93682 tow truck. (Mark Redman)

This 1945 Chevrolet 1-1/2-ton tow truck has been restored to its full military dress. (Bill Berg)

Both Kenworth and Ward LaFrance produced the classic 6-ton M1 6 x 6 giant. It could tow 70,000 lbs with its Garwood crane. This is the 1944 Ward LaFrance version. (John Gunnell)

This World War II Diamond T 969 is a 6 x 6 open-cab wrecker. The 4-tonner belongs to Ralph Doubek of Wild Rose, Wisconsin. (John Gunnell)

1920 and was widely advertised as the ideal solution for retrievals," Crismon noted. "The drum on the rear axle hub was for self-recovery winching."

By the World War II era, giant wreckers had been "enlisted" to "serve their country." A popular type was the "deuce-and-a-quarter" (2-1/2-ton) M60 built by REO. This 6 x 6 had a 20,000-lb., rear-mounted winch. It was essentially the same as the M108 (a crane truck utilizing the M35 cargo-truck chassis), but its platform was changed slightly so it could carry additional tools and equipment needed for salvage-and-recovery work. A revolving crane was mounted on the rear of the truck. It could swing 270 degrees between its stops on either side. The crane's capacity was 8,000 lbs. with its outriggers down and the boom elevated and retracted. With the boom extended, its capacity was "only" 4,000 lbs.

This ex-U.S. Navy crash truck is a 1962 Oshkosh with a Silent Hoist tow boom. In civilian dress white, it served Tolland Automotive of Hartford, Connecticut. (Mark Redman)

The Diamond T 969 was another huge wrecker. Development work on it began in 1939. It was built from 1940-1945. The 969 was a 6 x 6 heavy wrecker using a 106-hp 529-cid Hercules in-line six. The Model 45 wrecker body was built by the Ernest Holmes Co. The twin power booms could be swung out to the sides of the truck. These had a capacity of five tons each with the outriggers employed. Large quantities of recovery and hand tools, specialized recovery equipment, an air compressor and welding appliances were accessories.

Another World War II classic was the M1 wrecker. This 6 x 6 six-ton giant produced by both Kenworth and Ward LaFrance had a maximum towed load capacity of 70,000 lbs. The main part of the vehicle was a large Gar-Wood wrecker body with a heavy tow winch in the rear.

An A-frame main mast supported the overhanging boom. Boom-winch capacity was 16,000-20,000 lbs., depending on the model. It could lift about eight tons, but tow much more than that. A drag winch with 47,000-lb. capacity was located behind the large mast-and-boom.

Power for the M1 came from a 501-cid Continental 22R six with 145 hp. The M1A1, on the same chassis, featured an open military-style cab. Standard accessories included hand, vehicle and pioneer tools; spare parts; a fire extinguisher; welding and cutting tools; recovery equipment and salvage equipment. These rigs probably carried the most tools of any WWII trucks.

Another kind of battlefield recovery vehicle was a monster known as the Pacific M26A1 tractor. The 12-ton 6 x 6 truck was one of the largest used by the U.S. Army in World War II. If a tank broke down, this rig went got it—even in enemy territory. The M26A could scoop it up relatively quickly.

The M26A was a "crew-cab" semi-tractor with a 1090-cid Hall-Scott 440 six-cylinder engine generating 240 bhp. It carried a 40,000-lb. front winch and two 60,000-lb. winches at the rear of the frame, between the fifth-wheel

and cab. A boom-and-chain hoist was included for changing tires . . . the kind of job no one really looked forward to.

A tank could easily be loaded on the large M15A1 drop-frame semi-trailer. The center cargo deck that carried the tank was lower than the fifth-wheel unit. Eight large single combat wheels were used at the rear. Large hinged ramps were provided, too. When lowered, a tank could be pulled on to the trailer by the M26's rear winches. The 462-in. trailer was rated at 45 tons, but 60-100-ton loads could be hauled. These trailers weighed 42,370 lbs.

A second type of tank retriever was the M32B1, which looked like a tank itself. It was built on the M4 Sherman tank chassis and had the same basic configuration, but didn't carry a canon. It had a A-frame-type towing boom. These fully-tracked armored vehicles could recover an incapacitated tank in rough terrain, even under battle conditions.

These are only a few of the towing vehicles were used by America's Armed Services during World War II. If a khaki-green heavy-duty wrecker lights your fire, see if your library has a copy of Crismon's 472-page Crestline book.

A military surplus 6 x 6 wrecker was used by Hap Cramer's Mobil Service of Evanston, Illinois, in the early 1960s. (Hap Cramer)

A World War II-era Sterling featured dual chain drive. It served Naval aircraft in World War II, then was used by Lynch's Garage in Bordentown, New Jersey. (Mark Redman)

SHHH! THIS FEDERAL IS TOP SECRET! *By Tom Collins*

This story exposes a military secret—a true "Federal secret."

Early in 1940, the U.S. Army Air Force, as it was known before 1947, began preparing for what seemed inevitable American involvement in war.

Officials decided heavy lifting would be needed if B 17 or B 24 bombers lost their landing gear or belly flopped on a busy runway. A wrecker would have to be built to carry away crippled bombers to keep runways clear for other planes.

"The government specs came out requesting a 7.5 ton truck with a 10 ton swing boom crane," says investment banker and Federal restorer Tom Ratliff of Atlanta, Georgia.

Three manufacturers bid—Reo of Lansing, Michigan; Biederman of Cincinnati, Ohio; and Federal of Detroit—with Federal building most of the heavy trucks. That's where official records end.

"The government, under the Espionage Act of 1940, classified top secret all ground support for the [bombers]. That includes the Federal C2s," says Ratliff.

Some records have been obtained through Tom's attorney. They show the Federal was a 6 x 6 with a 60 quart cooling system, used air brakes and could hold 110 gallons of gas. Its gross weight was 40,500 pounds fully equipped with boom and 110 volt DC electric power for its flood lamps.

Tom says the C2 was powered by an 855 cid Hercules six-cylinder engine that gulped gas at a gluttonous slurp of one mile per gallon. The Federal was tortoise-like on highways.

"It would go 28 mph top speed downhill, wide open!" laughs Ratliff.

During the war, each Federal C2 cost about $35,000 but were sold for $2,000 to $2,500 on the surplus market following the war, often for use as tow trucks.

In 1975, a Federal from Central Garage in Titusville, Florida, helped NASA realign their shuttle booster missile's transport tracks.

Another Federal, owned by Ratliff and Sons of Sanford, Florida, Tom's dad, once went fishing, dead-lifting an entire 1950 Mercury sedan from deep water—complete with a fish swimming inside!

With just 9,000 miles on its odometer, Tom's Federal had been "hibernating" for several years in an old barn after its owner passed away. It was famous in the Carolinas for rescuing a bus and passengers that slid down a rugged mountainside one wintry day. Tom bought it from the late owner's wife.

The Federal C2s were powerful, durable vehicles in war and peace. The secret's out on this warrior turned towing giant.

In the 1950s, Ratliff and Sons wrecker service of Sanford, Florida, used a military surplus tow truck that retained its original aircraft recovery tow boom. (Thomas Ratliff)

The 1965 Chevrolet light duty truck catalog promoted this C3603 chassis-cab with a wrecker body added. The payload capacity was more than 6,100 lbs. (John Gunnell)

A 1998 Chevrolet with flat tow body is carrying a classic 1958 Chevy pickup with pride. (OCW)

This 1954 Chevrolet 4100 was coupled with a Weld Built wrecker when it was new. For many years, the Chevy served a Shell station in Queens, New York. (John Lee)

Gib Alper's 1927 Chevrolet began life as a farm truck but now is restored in tow truck form. It receives a lot of attention in the Fonda, Iowa, area. (Gib Alpers)

A vintage 1926 Ford Model TT tow truck stands next to contemporary tow trucks at Baker and Baker Towing in Woodburn, Oregon. (Roger Heinbach)

A veteran 1950s era Dodge "Pilot House" truck complete with dualies has been converted for tow truck use. Note the Packard Service logo on the door. (Roger Heinbach)

A tornado survivor, this Dodge Power Wagon was carefully preserved and now has a place of honor in the Dearth Chrysler-Dodge showroom in Monroe, Wisconsin. (Dearth photo)

John Stuppy is proud owner of this *1925 Canadian-built Ford Model TT*. It's an original and carries its working hand-cranked tow crane on back. *(John Stuppy)*

This dashing *1972 Ford four-wheel-drive COE* began life at Westover Air Force Base as a fire truck before becoming a tow truck at Roberts Towing of Glenmont, New York. *(Mark Redman)*

Wolleson's Garage of Calistoga, California, kept this "Owl Garage" *1931 Ford AA* in top condition. Note the unique roof-mounted beacon light and vintage wheel dolly. *(Roger Heinbach)*

On the lighter side, when Mr. Laurel and Mr. Hardy had trouble getting their *1924 Model T* pickup running, they called Herman's Garage and this *1930 Ford AA* tow truck came to the rescue. *(Herman Still)*

A late 1950s FWD tow truck carries a Weld Built tow body and crane. It stands out in yellow. (Ron Kowalke)

This 1936 GMC was on display at a St. Ignace, Michigan, truck show. It carries the Gray's Towing paint scheme and lettering. (John Gunnell)

Not the great pumpkin, this 1950s GMC 780 was decked out in orange for Lally's Garage of Swampscott, Massachusetts. (Mark Redman)

The 1937 Kenworthy GMC tow truck began life as a farm truck, then was mated with a vintage Manley tow unit. Now it's a beautiful "cover model" tow truck. (Kenworthy Truck and Auto Repair)

The 1975 International Paystar, owned by Northbrook Garage, and nicknamed "Monster II," always seems to be at the center of action—even at the carnival. (Jay Lorenz)

A shiny red 1993 Navistar 4700 might be mistaken for a new fire truck on first glance. It's owned by Mike's Auto and Towing, Windsor, Connecticut. (Mike Markesich)

A vintage 1952 Willys Jeep 1-ton truck gained second life as a tow truck thanks to the careful attention of Don Dugal of Woonsocket, Rhode Island. Note the coach lamps! (Don Dugal)

This 1950s Mack B61 with famed Thermodyne diesel engine was a mainstay for many tow operators. This one is "Back from Scrap" and ready for show. (Mack Truck Historical Archives)

New trucks were scarce in World War II until limited production was authorized in 1944. This Mack is a sturdy survivor of rare wartime civilian truck production. (OCW)

A late 1970s Mack R model tow truck poses at the gate of the Canadian National Exposition Grounds in Toronto, Ontario. This truck served DS Towing Service Ltd. (Mack Truck Historical Archives)

The Metzler family of Oshkosh, Wisconsin, owns this 1948 Nash tow truck. It's been on display at many car shows and its Nash Ambassador features always draw attention. (Don Metzler)

Mountain air was kind to this 1928 Studebaker, which worked for Marcus Motors, a Denver-area Studebaker dealer. It's complete with period oval headlights! (Van Horn Antique Truck Museum)

A rare 1935 Studebaker Ace tow truck and even rarer Marquette tow crane is owned by Ken Voigt, a Studebaker parts specialist from Armour, South Dakota. (Ken Voigt)

Bob Loudon of Ballwin, Missouri, owns this 1949 Nash tow truck. Nash built a limited number of tow trucks for dealers. (Bob Loudon)

A vintage red Brockway must have helped people remember Red and Art's Service Station of Stafford Springs, Connecticut. (Mark Redman)

The Arizona sunshine has been kind to Desert Air Salvage's 1940s era Diamond T tow truck. It looks fit and ready to work. (Roger Heinbach)

The Rehburger tow truck must have been a comforting image for travelers in distress during the late 1920s. It was "all truck," complete with its Manley tow crane. (Ron Kowalke)

This 1920 Reliable tow crane is about as rare as it gets. There's one other known to exist. Reliable cranes were built by Elite Manufacturing Co., Ashland, Ohio. (Donal Loker)

The Manley Manufacturing Company made tow equipment from as early as 1917 until 1985. This Manley unit is mounted on a 1920s Chevrolet. (Ron Kowalke)

A vintage Weaver chain hoist works just like it did when it was brand new. Owner Herman Still of Middletown, Pennsylvania, has kept it in excellent condition. (Herman Still)

A Weld Built tow body and crane was chosen for this 1954 Chevrolet chassis. The curved lines and single boom have graceful lines. A PTO drives the winch. (John Lee)

A little 1960s culture crept into this Holmes Retriever Wrecker ad with its "Dolly-a-Go-Go" self-loading dolly carried in back of a period Ford. (John Gunnell)

Here's a good look at a vintage hand-cranked Manley tow crane. It's mounted on a restored 1928 Model AA Ford. (Patrick Gilliam)

The Metzler Nash tow truck of Oshkosh, Wisconsin, is an example of the rare Nash tow trucks produced for franchised dealers only. (Metzler family)

Stallostown Towing is the name on the door of this beautiful 1920s Chevrolet tow truck. It carries a period-correct Manley tow unit on back. (Ron Kowalke)

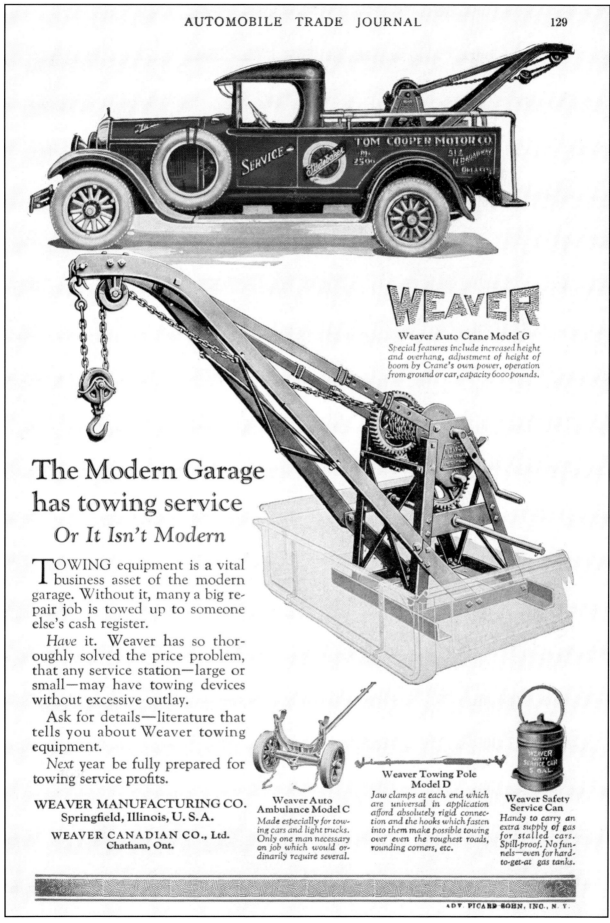

WEAVER

Weaver Auto Crane Model G

Special features include increased height and overhang, adjustment of height of boom by Crane's own power, operation from ground or car, capacity 6000 pounds.

The Modern Garage has towing service

Or It Isn't Modern

TOWING equipment is a vital business asset of the modern garage. Without it, many a big repair job is towed up to someone else's cash register.

Have it. Weaver has so thoroughly solved the price problem, that any service station—large or small—may have towing devices without excessive outlay.

Ask for details—literature that tells you about Weaver towing equipment.

Next year be fully prepared for towing service profits.

WEAVER MANUFACTURING CO.
Springfield, Illinois, U. S. A.

WEAVER CANADIAN CO., Ltd.
Chatham, Ont.

Weaver Auto Ambulance Model C

Made especially for towing cars and light trucks. Only one man necessary on job which would ordinarily require several.

Weaver Towing Pole Model D

Jaw clamps at each end which are universal in application afford absolutely rigid connection and the hooks which fasten into them make possible towing over even the roughest roads, rounding corners, etc.

Weaver Safety Service Can

Handy to carry an extra supply of gas for stalled cars. Spill-proof. No funnels—even for hard-to-get-at gas tanks.

ADV. PICARD-SOHN, INC., N. Y.

A Weaver ad from the 1920s shows all the equipment for the "modern garage" including the famed Auto Crane and the fully equipped Studebaker tow vehicle.

G and M Collision Repair Center features this authentic 1925 Ford Model T tow truck in their business. It carries a custom wooden cab and a Weaver tow crane. (Adrian and Terri Goodrich)

An aerial shot shows the red-colored vehicles in Hap Cramer's fleet—Chevrolets all in a row. (Hap Cramer)

Decked out in their festive finest, Hap Cramer's Chevrolet tow trucks pose in front of his Cities Service repair bays circa 1961. (Hap Cramer)

The tow crane chosen for the Rehburger was made by Manley. This truck is a well preserved gem from the earliest days of towing, more than 75 years ago. (Ron Kowalke)

This long-wheelbase Mack is a good example of today's impressive looking tow trucks. Its Century towing arm is used for heavy duty work. (Lanser Garage and Towing)

Three Chevy tow trucks in a row—a 1961, 1960 and 1959—and all part of the fleet of Hap Cramer. (Hap Cramer)

CHAPTER 5
SURVIVORS

1951 POWER WAGON TOW TRUCK IS A SURVIVOR

By John Gunnell

The slogan on Bob Dearth's business card says a lot about the 1951 Dodge Power-Wagon tow truck sitting inside the showroom at Dearth Motors, Inc., in Monroe, Wis. "Our 50 Year Reputation is Your Guarantee," the card says and the fully-restored, bright red Power Wagon has been helping to guarantee Dearth-style customer service practically since the Chrysler-Dodge dealership first opened.

According to Dearth, the truck — like the business — is a real survivor. It is one of two nearly identical tow trucks that the company once used to provide road service back in its formative years. At that time, Dearth handled all five brands represented by Chrysler's famous "pentastar" logo: Chrysler, Dodge, DeSoto, Imperial and Plymouth.

The truck not only survived a half-century of road calls and emergency service, it also survived an emergency that struck the dealership in the '60s. A tornado that tore through the city of Monroe leveled the Dearth dealership.

When the winds died down and the skies cleared, the building was little more than a pile of rubble. The only thing left intact after the storm was the Power Wagon. There was hardly a scratch on it.

Luckily, the truck's history has survived the years along with the vehicle itself. Copies of the Manufacturer's Statement of Origin and the original invoice for the vehicle are on display alongside the Power-Wagon in the company's modern showroom. They provide a unique glance at what it

The truck was in solid, original condition before a local craftsman restored it to its full and former glory, complete with bright red paint and appropriate lettering. (Angelo Van Bogart)

In September 2001, the Dodge Power-Wagon was fittingly displayed in the present-day dealership. (John Gunnell)

A 1960s tornado leveled the Dearth auto dealership in Monroe, Wisconsin. The 1951 Dodge Power Wagon survived and stood tall where it had been parked. (Dearth Motors)

took to put a well-equipped tow truck in service right after World War II.

The Manufacturer's Statement of Origin, certificate number T-410 states, "The undersigned corporation hereby certifies that the new motor vehicle described below (Invoice number 700124) is the property of said corporation and has been transferred this 5th day of Jan. 1950 to Dearth Motor Sales, whose address is Monroe, Wisc."

Many details about the Dodge are recorded on the MSO certificate (the predecessor of today's "window sticker"). The truck is described as follows: Trade Name: Dodge. Year: 1951. Series or Model: 82 PW. Body Type: Express. Number of Cylinders: 6. The document shows that the four-wheel-drive Power-Wagon had serial number 83920810 and was built with engine number T137 21129 (which it still carries). It was rated for 25.35 SAE net horsepower and had a shipping weight of 4,575 pounds.

The MSO was signed by the billing supervisor for Chrysler Corporation and listed the manufacturer's address as Chrysler Corporation, Detroit, Mich. The original invoice adds the name of the Dodge Division and the Detroit postal code, which was "31."

Invoice number 700124 gives some of the same information, as well as additional facts about the truck's history. It specifies that the Power-Wagon was delivered from Detroit to Monroe, Wis., by common carrier and financed by Interstate Finance Corporation of Dubuque, Iowa. Its List Number was 1015 and the serial number and motor number match those previously noted, as does the invoice date of Jan. 5, 1950.

Perhaps the most interesting thing reflected by the invoice is the breakdown of the truck's equipment and the cost of each item. The basic truck itself had a factory price of $1,554. It had 10 accessories related to its being outfitted for tow truck service. The most expensive extra was a complete hydraulic lift, which cost Dearth Motors $439.70. The tow winch was the second priciest accessory and listed for $152. The pulley added $55.45, a tailshaft setup added $54.70 and the power take-off was priced at $49.40. A governor cost $47.75, the tow type body was only $22.80, an overdrive gear cost $4.55, printle-type tow hooks set Dearth Motors back $3.80 and outside mirrors added $3.75 to the price. In total, the accessories added $943.10 to the cost of the basic truck.

There were a few other costs and taxes, which were the highest on the hydraulic lift. The invoice separately noted a "provision for federal taxes" for the truck ($85.25) and the accessories ($49.20). In addition, Dearth Motors paid $20 for corporate advertising, $5 for the Dodge Forward Fund, $5 for special delivery service, $1 for antifreeze service and 25-cents for the MSO certificate. All of this plus a little more brought the grand total for a new four-wheel-drive tow truck to all of $2,663.

If you think $2,663 for a new, fairly heavy-duty tow truck sounds like a great value, consider the value that Dearth Motors has realized over the truck's 51-year history. It works out to a cost of $52.22 per year for the dealership's long-lasting "survivor."

Dearth Motors offered "day and night service" in the 1950s. Stranded motorists only had to dial three numbers to reach help. (John Gunnell)

ROAD SERVICE RELICS

By John Gunnell

Over the past few months I've been collecting photos of tow trucks to feature in this book. Several co-workers who traveled to car shows across the country, and friends who took their cameras along on their vacations this year, were nice enough to snap tow truck photos for me. Quite a few of these vehicles might be called "road service relics" — dilapidated tow trucks parked in weeds, in salvage yards or behind old repair shops.

It's clear that old tow trucks have something in common with old soldiers — they never die, they just fade, fade away. That's good news for those of us with a passion for the old beasts, since it means there still are trucks left to restore. Let's look at some basics involved in the "art" of restoring an older truck.

No junk!

First, you will need a tow truck to restore. Stay away from junkers and clunkers. Restoring any vehicle is an expensive, labor-intensive effort. Parts will be the biggest expense. Most hobbyists rebuilding an old engine can hold down the costs of disassembly, machining, painting and re-assembly to around $900. The parts needed to rebuild that same engine may run as high as $1,600. The fewer parts you need, the easier the job and the lower the expense.

The same is with body work. An old fender with only surface rust, dents or paint damage can be fixed, but a rusted-out fender has to be replaced. Finding a replacement may be hard and paying for it even harder. Look for a truck with solid parts that can be repaired. Rust (other than

surface rust that can be chemically dissolved) is the restorer's worst enemy.

How much to pay

There are price guides to old-car values. Most of these books and magazines cover pickup truck values, not tow truck prices. In general, the smaller the truck, the more it's worth to collectors. This is simply a function of the law of supply and demand. Many collectors don't have enough room to store big trucks, so more people want the small ones.

It would still be a good idea to purchase a copy of *Old i*

Gib Alpers poses with his restored 1927 Chevrolet. You can see it at the Fonda Opera House Museum in Fonda, Iowa. (Dale Garlock/ Buena Vista Co. Journal)

This beautiful 1927 Chevrolet wrecker was originally a dilapidated farm truck. It is part of the collection at the Gib Alpers Fonda Opera House Museum in Fonda, Iowa. (Dale Garlock/ Buena Vista Co. Journal)

Gilbert Alpers located a 1920s-style hand-cranked Weaver wrecking boom and installed it on his Chevrolet. The truck was lettered by a Spencer, Iowa, professional sign painter. (Gilbert Alpers)

John Sawruk, a former General Motors engineer, spotted this 1940s Chevrolet tow truck while he was vacationing in Victor, Colorado, an old mining town. (John Sawruk)

The Chevrolet looks like a great restoration project because all parts are there and it isn't a victim of severe rust. (John Sawruk)

Donal Loker of Penn Laird, Virginia, has restored several Ford tow trucks. A current project is this 1932 Ford and Holmes 110 tow boom. (Donal Loker)

This 1960s-era Chevrolet tow truck seems very worthy of taking out of the weeds and restoring. (Ron Kowalke)

to use the pickup truck prices as a general guide. As a rule of thumb, deduct 10-15 percent from the listed prices to determine what to offer for that old tow truck.

Keep in mind that rarity doesn't always add value. Parts for a rare vehicle are harder to find and this makes restoring such a rig more expensive. Also, some vehicles are rare because they had less appeal when they were new. Maybe poor styling or mechanical problems made them unpopular. In any case, a restored example will still have the same problems.

Do-it-yourself

As a tow-truck operator, you probably have some familiarity with auto repairs. That doesn't mean you'll have all the skills it takes to do a proper restoration, but you should be able to do some of the work yourself and save money in the process. Let's say you want a top-notch paint job on your old tow truck. You'll hire the best painter in town to spray the truck, and you can probably handle the removal of chrome trim, surface preparation of the metal and possibly even applying the primer. Any work you can do will save you money.

Do-it-yourself operations can save when it comes to mechanical work, too. For example, restorers usually charge $300 to $350 just to remove an engine before rebuilding it. If you take out the engine yourself, you're that much ahead of the game.

Join a truck club

Joining a club that covers the type of vehicle you're restoring is an essential step. Most clubs are organized to help members exchange information and parts through regular newsletters. Usually, members can place ads in such publications free of charge.

Two clubs stand out as "the places" for restorers of old trucks. The Antique Truck Club of America, PO Box 291,

Hershey, PA 17033, was founded in 1971 for commercial vehicle owners and those with an interest in the preservation and restoration of older trucks. It publishes Double Clutch magazine six times a year. The club's Website www.atca-inc.net includes an online membership form that can be used to sign up electronically.

Another great organization for truck restorers is the American Truck Historical Society, PO Box 901611, Kansas City, MO 64190-1611.

They publish Wheels of Time magazine on a bi-monthly basis and maintain a library and archives related to commercial vehicle history. Their Web address is www.aths.org.

Both of these clubs can help you find, fix up and have fun with that old tow truck you spotted in that farmer's field last week. The next step is up to you.

Here's a mid-1940s Ford tow truck just waiting for the right person to restore it. While worn, it's in very restorable condition. A restorable Studebaker stands next to it. (John Gunnell)

FORD MODEL TT MATCHES HISTORIC MISSOURI COMMUNITY

By Tom Collins

Ste. Genevieve, Missouri, is a living reminder of the uniquely beautiful French culture that pioneered this region, one hour south of St. Louis and nestled on the Mississippi River.

It's appropriate that John and Mary Stuppy decided to honor their towing firm's legacy with a venerable 1925 Model TT Ford, part of automotive legend. The Canadian-built Ford came to the Stuppys from British Columbia.

"John was looking for something different to celebrate being in wrecker service for 35 years. He was looking on e-Bay and came across this great find," says Mary Stuppy. "We were happy to find it in good running condition and fully operational."

The white and red-accented hand-cranked tow unit contrasts with the basic black Ford.

The Stuppys have added wooden rails above the truck's box that advertise their firm and its location.

In 1925, a Ford Model TT without a body could range from $365 to $430, depending on the truck's weight. Ford began producing both a roadster pickup and closed cab pickup that year. Many Model Ts and TTs wore bodies that were produced locally by a number of body makers.

There is a special history in Stuppy Auto Body and Wrecker Service. Thomas Stuppy began the business in 1968, then suddenly died. His brothers, John and Ronald, kept the business going and have recently been joined by a third brother, Scott.

Stuppy Auto Body and Wrecker Service has a reputation in Missouri for service and quality.

Ste. Genevieve values a rich heritage, something that has taken root in the Stuppy family's auto body and towing operation. John couldn't have chosen a better symbol for his business and community than this striking '25 Ford Model TT.

Nearing its 80th birthday, the Canadian-built 1925 Ford Model TT still looks ready to work. (John Stuppy)

Imagine the stories of towing history this Canadian '25 Ford Model TT could tell about vehicles it may have rescued and towed through the years. It's a rolling survivor of tow truck history. (John Stuppy)

MODEL T TOW TRUCK HONORED AT ITS FLORIDA RETIREMENT HOME *By John Gunnell*

"Snowbirds" come from the northern United States and portions of Canada to enjoy Florida's warm air and sunny beaches. Many decide to stay. It's fitting that an elderly Ford Model T tow truck, 1925 vintage, has relocated to Key West, Florida.

Adrian and Terri Goodrich of G and M Collision Center have restored and respected this "retiree," making it the centerpiece of their firm's lobby.

The Ford and Weaver tow unit has always been a tow truck. The Model T's cab was custom-made for the Model T chassis by U. S. Hame Company of Buffalo, New York. The wrecker worked in Pennsylvania and in 1975, moved on to Detroit, Michigan, where it appeared in parades.

Adrian and Terri brought the Model T into the warm sunshine of Key West in the 1990s. There the Model T's original wooden cab, body and tow crane all received a lot of care.

Today the Ford greets customers and visitors amid a mural of its past and an array of tools and parts, a tremendous homage to the history of the towing and auto body industry. Long life to you in retirement, old veteran!

This 1925 Ford Model T has found a good home in the lobby of G and M Collision Center of Key West, Florida, reminding visitors of the towing industry's rich past. (Adrian and Terri Goodrich)

CHAPTER 6
TOW STORIES

SAWALLICH GARAGE DID IT ALL

By John Gunnell

Harry Sawallich was born in 1911. By the ripe old age of 18 or 19, he was working at the Ford dealership in Howell, Michigan. In those days, the auto repair industry employed "mechanics," rather than "service technicians." For many young men in rural areas, fixing cars was natural. It offered a good career choice.

Take Kenny Huff for example. He helped Harry tear down more than a few Model A Ford engines and put them back together. Kenny also knew his away around tractors and agricultural machinery. He grew up on a farm and continued to work it even after being hired at the Ford agency. But, Huff always figured that fixing one of "Henry's Ladies" inside a cozy dealership garage was easier than cranking a tractor to plow snow on a cold winter morning.

Shorty Woodward also helped Harry Sawallich get those Model As running right. Later, Woodward would become parts manager at the Ford garage, which seemed to him like cleaner work. Another member of the talent pool was Earl Smith, who also found the auto repair trade a good business to work in during the Great Depression.

The ever-changing car repair business went through transitions in those years, too. Eventually, the Ford agency moved across the street. The dealership building where Harry had worked became a Cadillac and Oldsmobile garage. (Amazingly, the building survives today as Budget Tire Co.) Young new mechanics came into the workforce. Veterans like Harry Sawallich decided they could make better money running their own repair shops. And many of the

In early 1940s, Harry Sawallich purchased his 1937 Ford truck at a farm auction for $300. He was a talented mechanic and body man who did the tow truck conversion himself. (Albert Sawallich)

independent shops, including Harry's, began entering the sideline business of towing damaged or broken-down automobiles.

Harry called his shop in Howell the Sawallich Garage. He advertised general repairing, bumping (body work), painting and 24-hour wrecker service. The name Sawallich Garage was proudly lettered on the doors of his 1937 Ford 1-1/2-ton wrecker, along with the three-digit daytime telephone number 960. Also included in ads was his night number, 649.

Sawallich bought his truck in 1942 or 1943 at a farm auction. He paid the princely sum of $300 for it. In its first life, the '37 Ford had been a farm truck and its hard-working background showed.

When his son Albert first saw the Ford, he told his father, "It looks like it's been in a wreck itself!"

The paint was badly faded and the fenders were in terrible shape, but Harry Sawallich was pretty talented. He knew he could have the six-year-old truck looking like new in no time.

Harry went back to see Shorty Woodward in the dealership parts department. He ordered a set of new fenders for the '37 Ford. Then, he rebuilt a 1939 Mercury flathead V-8 engine and installed it under the hood. A winch made by Gar-Wood Industries, of Detroit, was acquired. The boom was fabricated by Henry Wilmer, a local fellow who was an absolute master at welding.

The truck needed some rear fenders, so Harry found a Fordson tractor in a junkyard down the street from his shop that was happy to donate a set. He then painted his wrecker with shiny black paint and finished the fenders in contrasting white. The boom was spray painted aluminum. By that time the truck was looking great and it performed to

match its appearance.

"My dad had a very successful business," Albert Sawallich recalls. "He ran it all by himself."

The old Ford truck served him well, until the fateful day, in 1948, when a dump truck crashed and wound up in someone's basement. Harry chained his wrecker to a tree to winch a Dodge out. The technique worked and got the job done, but it also bent the frame of the tow truck.

After that, Harry Sawallich bought a new 1948 Ford F-5 truck and fitted the old boom to it. He then sold the 1937 Ford truck to a man who had a welding shop. Albert doesn't know what happened to the original tow truck after that, but the new Ford made a fine replacement.

24 **Hour Wrecker Service** 24

Phone Howell, Nights 649, Days 960

Sawallich Garage, Howell, Michigan

General Repairing, - Bumping - Painting

The Sawallich Garage was located at 219 N. National in Howell, Michigan. Amazingly, the building is still standing and Harry's wife still lives there. This is an early ad for the business. (Albert Sawallich)

The Ford garage, filled with Model As, as it looked in 1928 or 1929. Harry Sawallich is on the left, next to Shorty Woodward. then comes "farmer" Kenny Huff and Earl Smith is on the far right. (Albert Sawallich)

THE BIG WRECKER ON MY ROAD

By Jack M. Sheridan

Each year I treat myself to a trip back to my native Washington to visit friends and relatives. Invariably, I find myself on Interstate 5, between Portland and Seattle. I retreat to the solitude and tranquility along sections of Old Highway 99, the two-lane predecessor of the interstate. And I reminisce.

While traveling between Mary's Corner and Toledo (on a section now called the Jackson Highway), my car was nearly alone on the road and it became difficult to visualize when this section was the main highway. It was always clogged with cars, huge trucks and lumbering buses.

As a child living in Seattle, during the 1940s, I took a personal interest in Highway 99, particularly the stretch between Tenino and Kelso. At least twice a year, my family trekked to Longview to visit my grandparents and bunches of relatives living nearby.

Traveling in an always-shiny, two-toned 1940 Pontiac sedan, I was a keen observer of things along the highway. After awhile, I figured that I knew that concrete strip as well as anyone and it became "my" road.

Starting the journey south from Seattle was always exciting. My two sisters and I would decide what might be the focus for our trip. Sometimes we directed our attention exclusively on Burma Shave signs, memorizing any new jingles or rhymes.

Kemp Olson is at the wheel of his 1928 Fageol, prepared for service along then new Highway 99. The Fageol, complete with axe and lanterns, announces "Service Day and Night." The phone number was 193. (Olson family)

The Olson Brothers' Central Garage in Toledo, home to the Fageol that delighted author Jack Sheridan as a boy. The garage began operations in 1926 and still exists, though it's not a garage. (Olson family)

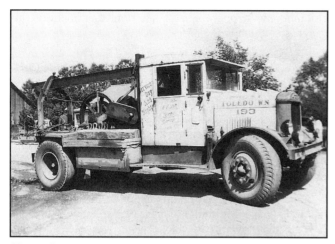

If you listen closely enough, the 1928 Fageol beckons everyone who loved trucks as a boy or girl to come closer. Come explore! (Olson family)

Sometimes we'd speculate about the causes of the Tenino mystery mounds. (We usually decided they had to be burial mounds.) And we would play the alphabet game, taking the letters off license plates and billboards.

Sometimes our focus was a tally of the wrecks we'd spot along the way. Highway 99 always was crowded with traffic and driving it became an adventure. Our plan was to arrive in Longview with a list of vehicular mishaps so our young cousins would listen, wide-eyed, to descriptions of the carnage we had witnessed.

During all the times that we traveled that congested roadway, I don't recall seeing a single major accident. There were fender benders now and then, but it was difficult for us to embellish our descriptions very much.

Probably the worst accident we ever encountered, was the time some guy lost a load of household goods when his open, two-wheeled trailer overturned. Having to swerve around a lampshade in the middle of Highway 99 provided grist for an exaggerated tale of misfortune.

Longview always was our destination, but we often visited relatives along the way. One place where we particularly enjoyed stopping was Toledo where Kemp and Esther Olson, and their daughter Darlene, lived in a house on the banks of the Cowlitz River. Esther was my mother's cousin. In my young mind's eye, there were other good reasons for stopping in Toledo!

Kemp Olson and his brothers owned and operated a large garage a block from the family's home. Since I had already developed a deep love affair with cars and trucks, that garage was equivalent to the Taj Mahal. The scene was made even closer to "heaven on earth" by a large lot separating the garage from the house. It was always strewn with broken and wrecked vehicles which were there because Kemp also operated a large Fageol wrecker. To me, that massive tow truck was Toledo's centerpiece.

The big Fageol wrecker usually was parked away from the house, to be admired only from a distance. One sunny afternoon, as we slipped down the gravel road to their house, my eyes opened wide. The big wrecker was parked only yards away! My heart skipped a beat and my mind went into high gear! Now was my chance to bond with that magnificent behemoth! ("Biggest wrecker on the West

Coast!" I would brag to my Seattle friends.)

As we clambered from the Pontiac, I asked my mother if I could spend a few minutes with the object of my affection. I gulped as she turned and peered down at me with her familiar motherly frown. I quickly remembered that my mother believed that all little boys, no matter how mild mannered or innocent looking, performed acts of great destruction.

Surely, Mother was thinking her young son's nearness to that great wrecker would result in its untimely demise; as if I might somehow send it reeling end over end, down the river bank, into the flowing Cowlitz!

Mother had been the oldest child in a large family that included four brothers who were often bent on challenging or compromising her rank. I returned her immediately disapproving expression with a pitiful look of merciful begging.

Seeking help from other family members was futile. In matters such as this, my father always played a passive, detached role. Aside from that, his interest was in trains, not the trucks that he often cursed vehemently as we traveled along Highway 99.

My older sister could be a strong ally, but she was also the one who frequently recited that galling childhood poem about ". . . snails and puppy dog tails!" At this crucial time, I didn't feel she could be trusted.

My "little" sister was too young to be of much help. Besides, if she became interested, I would have had to take her with me. It would be intolerable to have your little sister involved in a very private and manly affair. As usual, it was all up to my mother.

I cringed when she took a deep breath, usually a precursor of some dire pronouncement. "Well, OK," she said, still frowning. "But, don't touch anything!"

I was momentarily stunned, but quickly recovered and began sidestepping away from my family. The time-honored tactic was to move out of hearing range as quickly as possible. It worked.

The 1928 Fageol now is retired from service and protected from vandalism in this fenced enclosure. It's a survivor of more than 35 years of service. (Olson family)

Moments later I was with the giant wrecker that plied "my" road, hauling in disabled cars, trucks and buses. But I could not be overjoyed for ". . . don't touch anything!" echoed in my mind like a bad headache. I knew there could not be bonding without touching or feeling.

Positioning myself directly in front of the wrecker, I stood far enough back to stare upward into its massive windshield. Never before had I felt so awestruck. Years ago, the truck had been delivered with gleaming white paint, but the grime and sweat of time on the road had faded its white finish and its red lettering. The big truck appeared proud and invincible, ready for action in a flash. I could not imagine an object of greater beauty and utility.

Like many boys, I believed in the animate nature of most things — especially cars and trucks. All of my toy vehicles had lives and names. The family Pontiac spent most of its life parked in a basement suite directly below our living room. In my presence, the big Fageol wrecker assumed life.

It sent signals only I could interpret. It beckoned me to step closer. It agreed wholeheartedly to a conspiracy of touching. If I was to eventually stand trial, it agreed to being a co-defendant.

I acted with extreme caution. Receiving a long jail sentence was one thing and facing my mother's wrath was quite another. I knew that the latter could happen first — and be far more consequential. Looking back towards the house, I noted everyone had gone inside. My mother wasn't staring sternly at me from the window.

My next thought was that I could discreetly place my hand on the truck's massive bumper. A mocking, admonishing signal from the truck interceded. "That won't do it!" it seemed to declare. So, hesitantly, I slipped to the side of the truck away from the house and I stepped boldly up onto the running board.

Energy from the truck started flowing into my body. I felt empowered like never before. Peering into the cab, with its maze of levers and a mammoth steering wheel, I imagined the Fageol driving itself with me on the running board giving it signals to turn and adjust its speed. I knew that we would be invincible as a team. People would look on in awe as the boy on the wrecker whizzed by on a mission of rescue.

All Fageol trucks of that era had an intriguing design feature that consisted of six rear-facing fin louvers. They looked like saw teeth on the center of the hood. Standing on the running board, I decided that it was possible for me to reach over and touch the saw teeth. I thought it would complete the bonding process.

As I leaned to reach upward, I stopped. I remembered I was dressed in my Sunday school clothes. There was a possibility of dirt from the truck soiling me as I pressed against it. With reluctance, I decided to instead grip the door handle, before stepping onto the gravel below the truck.

Back at the house, as I expected, my mother eyed me suspiciously and glanced outside, as if to insure I had done no harm. I received the same look when I went to the bathroom, where I washed away an almost indistinguishable layer of dust acquired during the bonding experience.

Returning to the living room, I sat quietly, like a model child, hoping no one would ask questions that might reveal my errant behavior.

As the Pontiac eased away, I looked back through the rear window and smiled at the giant wrecker. Naturally, it cast back a wry, knowing grin.

We're still friends! The 1928 Fageol remains in operable condition at Moses Lake, Washington. During 1998, my "little" sister and I located the truck and its current owner, Larry Fowler. Larry was a partner with the Olson brothers for a time. The wrecker is still lettered "Olson Brothers, Inc."

Sadly, the truck and I didn't communicate as we once had so long ago. My ability to engage in animation somehow faded during my early adolescence. The truck also appeared to be much smaller than it was. Many things from my boyhood have gone through this same amazing transition.

The big tow truck is still in operating condition, but it is not for hire. It hasn't been licensed since 1976. Larry says he used it much less after 1965.

The section of Highway 99 that ran through Toledo had been completed in 1923. Kemp Olson, who undertook operation of his garage in 1926, decided there was a need for a heavy-duty tow truck on Highway 99.

The 1928 Fageol began its life as a freight truck. Kemp bought the truck and rebuilt it, adding a homemade wrecker boom. For a time, it was the largest wrecker in use between Seattle and Portland.

The giant Fageol could handle the huge trucks and buses that broke down on Highway 99 and on other roads around Toledo. Kemp quickly discovered his wrecker could also be useful in other ways. If a local logger lost his load along the roadway, the wrecker could be pressed into service. A telling photograph shows the truck's tow boom lifting a light aircraft that was damaged during the Columbus Day storm of 1962.

The big wrecker on "my" road was a great tow truck and a major operator for at least 35 years.

We see the back of a "squashed" 1953 Chevrolet that has been towed into Toledo by the Fageol wrecker sometime in the early 1950s.(Olson family)

OHIO TOWING FIRM WAS A FAMILY AFFAIR

By Tom Collins

For many years, if you needed breakdown service in the North Ridgeville, Ohio, area the people you called were named Gilder. Ralph Gilder began an auto repair service in North Ridgeville in 1920, taking one half of the barn used by his dad, Charlie, a blacksmith. Originally, Ralph towed with a team of horses before buying a roadster-style 1922 Atlas truck mounted with a towing boom.

Like many early mechanics, Ralph used his blacksmith's background to fabricate equipment and adapt to ideas for car repair. And Charlie's blacksmithing knowledge was always helpful.

"Grandpa was a walking mechanic," recalls grandson Bob Gilder.

By 1931, Gilder and Son had been awarded the AAA service franchise for their area, and served the police, sheriff and the Ohio State Patrol over the next 37 years.

Eventually, the Atlas was replaced by a late '20s Packard.

"When I was a kid, the Packard used to sit in back of the garage, " recalls Bob. "I used to sit and play in it and turn the wheel."

In the mid '30s, the Gilders bought a '31 Chevrolet four-cylinder 1 1/2 ton wrecker that fell victim to an accident itself. In 1943, it was hit on Ohio Route 20 and reportedly smashed to pieces. The Chevy had used the boom from the retired Atlas.

The Chevy's replacement was a '37 Ford, purchased from a trucking company and coupled with the old boom from the '31 Chevy's remains. Ralph decided to move up from a hand-cranked winch and fabricated a power unit.

After World War II, Charlie Gilder had passed on. Bob joined his dad and brother "Murph" (Don) in the business. "Murph" was a student at Cleveland's Baldwin-Wallace College and later worked for Chevrolet in the Cleveland area.

As the world changed in the post-war years, so did the Gilder's business. By 1956, they had been running a Studebaker wrecker for a number of years and decided to invest in some other wreckers including a 1948 White WA-22 in which a military half track "Mustang" engine was inserted. The engine been crated as WWII surplus.

"That old White was tired but that engine gave it new life," recalls Bob. "We made it stand tall and we were in business!"

During World War II new trucks were impossible to get. Ralph Gilder, at the wheel, repaired a 1937 Ford and built his own automated tow boom. (Bob Gilder)

Gilder brothers Bob (top) and Don began in front of their dad's repair shop with their own 1935 Gilder—a car they made from a packing box and spare wheels. (Bob Gilder)

The Gilders were known for the colonial gray and red-painted tow trucks.

In 1957, the Gilder's added a one ton Chevrolet to the fleet. By 1960, they switched from the original site and operated their towing service out of the town's Shell station where they also repaired cars.

Eventually, their AAA sanctioned fleet included a heavy duty '46 Ward LaFrance three ton, a '57 White COE two ton, a '59 GMC 1 1/2 ton and a '63 Chevrolet one ton.

The Ward LaFrance came in handy winching Autocar coal hauling trucks and trailers that became stuck in massive coal piles at the Cleveland area CEI power plant.

"If the 'dozer didn't get the coal packed down, we'd have to go out and winch those trucks off the coal pile," laughs Bob. "They got in a lot of trouble on nights and weekends when that 'dozer wasn't working!"

In 1963, as America's important highways were turned into expressways and turnpikes, Gilder's received a contract to cover a 30 mile stretch of the Ohio Turnpike.

After 48 years in the family business built by their father and grandfather, the Gilder brothers decided it was time to park their trucks for the last time and let someone else take over the "24-7-365" demand for towing and motor services.

After years of volunteering, Bob had a chance to join North Ridgeway's new full-time fire department in 1968. He and Murph, who also was being transferred to GM in Detroit, decided to sell off their fleet. For a brief time, Bob

In 1920, Ralph Gilder took half of dad Charlie Gilder's blacksmith shop and started a garage. Ralph's first tow truck, a 1922 Atlas, used a tow boom he and his dad crafted. (Bob Gilder)

This version of the Gilder's fleet includes (left to right) a 1956 International L 190 2-1/2 ton, a 1966 Chevrolet 1-1/2 ton and a 1967 Chevrolet 1-ton. (Bob Gilder)

Bob (left) and Don "Murph" Gilder pose in front of their 1965 Chevrolet 50 1-1/2 ton tow truck with Holmes 535 booms. (Bob Gilder)

did some long-distance towing in his spare time.

Along the way, three generations of Gilders had been involved in the business.

"I saw every kind of damage a person could do to a vehicle," Bob said reflectively. "It always was a personal business."

The Gilders had seen all kinds of recovery work and even had to chase turkeys in the aftermath of one accident!

They had grown and expanded in their business just as the automobile had taken hold in the nation over nearly a half century. It was an unforgettable journey.

The Gilder's fleet early in the 1960s included (left to right) a 1946 Ward LaFrance 3-ton, a 1957 White COE 2-ton, a 1959 GMC 1-1/2 ton and a 1962 Chevrolet 1-ton. (Bob Gilder)

CHAPTER 7
TOW TRUCKS IN ACTION

NORTHBROOK GARAGE

By Tom Collins

If the telephone was available when Clem and Henry Studebaker upgraded the family's South Bend, Indiana, blacksmith shop to their new business of making wagons in 1852, they might have called a Northbrook, Illinois, shop for advice.

That's because Frederick Lorenz' business was more than nine-years-old when the Studebakers were beginning their venture.

Their shop has grown with the changing nation, progressing from blacksmithing to early auto and truck body making to heavy duty towing and vehicle leasing.

Now more than five generations and 160-years-old, Northbrook Garage has seen Studebaker wagons, cars and trucks all come into prominence and pass into history while their business continues to flourish.

Tow drivers never know what they'll be hauling next. Here, the Northbrook Garage 1936 Ford "Mighty Mouse" prepares to pull dual milk trailers. (Jay Lorenz)

A YOUNG TOW MAN OF EVANSTON

By Tom Collins

In the late '50s, a gas station job brought many teens closer to the cars they enjoyed. One example was Allan "Hap" Cramer, the proud owner of a '55 Corvette V8. Hap worked at a Pure Station in Wilmette, Illinois, a Chicago suburb, and dreamed of owning a service station. For this hard worker, it was a natural. At age 22, in 1960, he leased a Mobil station and bought a used tow truck. Then he got into trouble

In Illinois, tow vehicles could bring in vehicles to their own stations but couldn't tow for hire without ICC certification. A competitor, Miller Brothers, blew the whistle on Hap. After some legal wrangling, he was able to get his ICC certification.

Soon, the whistle blower was whistling a different tune. Johnny Miller offered young Hap a chance to buy the Miller towing business. While he got the young entrepreneur's new Cadillac as part of the down payment, the towing business was now Hap's to control.

Hap moved down the street to an Arrow Station, which soon became a Cities Service station, and became very busy.

"We provided 24-7 service," says Hap. "I was single and working 7 days a week and spent money buying fancy cars…but never had a chance to drive them much. Usually I was in the tow truck."

"In cold weather, we'd close the station at 10 p.m. and still have 100 tows to go on."

Hap owned Corvettes, Thunderbirds and Cadillacs plus motorcycles but at least one tow truck, a 1961 Chevrolet Viking 60, had a little something extra. It was powered by a Corvette V8 and sported Chevrolet Super Sport bucket seats from the era. And Hap said the Chevy had a great set of air horns he enjoyed using!

Hap got the lucrative contract to tow stolen and abandoned cars from the City of Evanston.

"We towed the cars off the street. They sat for 90 days at the impound yard," he recalls. "The cars were advertised and then had to be scrapped if they were unclaimed."

Hap was in the tow business for five years, went in police work in Deerfield, Illinois, and then became a Lake County Sheriff's Department detective. Today he's working in land development. "I'd like to get into the tow truck business again today, but then I'm 65 now, too. It was a demanding job in the tow business."

He remembers the cars and the fun he had, as well as the hard work. The adventurous Hap also has owned an Auburn Supercharged boat-tail speedster and flown an airplane. This young man never has stopped pursuing his dreams.

City tow trucks often impound abandoned or illegally parked cars. In the 1960s, these cars went to salvage when they were unclaimed within a specified time. (Hap Cramer)

WRECKERS IN ACTION

On Columbus Day, 1962, a storm devastated portions of western Washington. The 1928 Fageol is working to retrieve a small plane from wreckage near Toledo, Washington. (Olson family)

The Northbrook Garage's "Might Mouse" 1936 Ford also towed its own bus on an occasional sightseeing trip. (Jay Lorenz)

Trains can be dangerous to their own maintenance vehicles! This Union Pacific work truck was on the wrong track when it was hit at 60-mph. (Jay Lorenz)

Some tow trucks are called on to rescue a beer delivery truck in trouble. That gives a new meaning to "Miller time." (Jay Lorenz)

Veteran tower Jay Lorenz shows what can happen when a car, in this case a 1959 Chevrolet, is impaled at high speed on a guard rail. (Jay Lorenz)

The pizza guy's Freightliner had an accident on this wintry day and the heavy duty International tow truck came to the rescue. (Henry Vanden Heuvel)

Versatile tow trucks often do more than pulling and hauling. This *1959 Chevrolet Viking 50* became a steel erecting crane using special pole attachments. (Henry Vanden Heuvel)

A *1959 Chevrolet Viking 50* uses a towing dolly to transport a vintage touring sedan in 1961. (Henry Vanden Heuvel)

A World War II era GMC prepares to pull a truck full of steel from a soft shoulder in 1948. (Jay Lorenz)

Trains can really give a truck a bad day. Here's a late '40s Dodge COE being towed after its encounter with a train at Morton Grove, Illinois. (Jay Lorenz)

The 1963 Chevrolet station wagon driver was killed when his car swerved and couldn't recover in time. It hit the oncoming tow truck at full speed. (Henry Vanden Heuvel)

CHAPTER 8
AT YOUR SERVICE

A GOOD APRIL FOOL'S DAY IDEA

By John Gunnell

The launching of the California State Automobile Association's Emergency Road Service has to be one of the best things that ever happened on the first day of April. Unlike the many gags related to that date, the ERS was a serious program aimed at helping motorists should "Lady Luck" decide to play jokes on them.

ERS was offered in four California cities: San Francisco, Oakland, Berkeley and Alameda. It used a fleet of yellow-and-blue tow cars and motorcycles manned by expert mechanics and troubleshooters. In 1924, Louis Signer was hired to organize the ERS department. "Signer was my boss," said George Conway in 1999. Conway started working at CSAA during the early days of Emergency Road Service and dispatched road-service trucks until 8 p.m.

"I'd sit at the switchboard and open the door with a release switch," he explained. "In the evenings there'd be quite a few people walking up and down Van Ness Ave., auto row back then. They would be looking at the cars through showroom windows. If someone looked interested, I'd buzz them in. You'd be surprised how many memberships I sold that way."

Conway was such a dedicated employee that, when he got through working in the evening, he'd sometimes ride along to find out just what happened on a road-service call. Sometimes he'd get a ride home that way too.

"They didn't call it Emergency Road Service when we started," Conway recalled. "It was Mechanical First Aid and Towing Service. The name changed to ERS shortly after we moved to 150 Van Ness.

As young as I was at the time, I was one of the advocates to change the name. I don't know why they started out with Mechanical First Aid—maybe to be different."

By the spring of 1924, the CSAA sold auto insurance, maps and touring information, erected road signs, lobbied for better roads and offered free legal advice to members. Nothing was more important than emergency road service. When a car breaks, having help on the way is a godsend.

"Originally there were several service limitations that were later removed," George Conway explained.

This car, believed to be mid-1920s Lincoln, was converted for use as a service car by the California State Automobile Association. (John Gunnell)

"Service was confined to a radius of 10 miles from the nearest contract station. Tire change service was not provided for able-bodied men. Many members would have their wives or lady friends call for service and then stay out of sight until the tire was changed."

The CSAA operated 22 branch offices in 1924 and served 26,000 members. The office on San Francisco's auto row, between California and Sacramento streets, was its headquarters. Louis Singer remained in charge until he retired at the end of 1945. William Haley then took his place and George Conway became assistant ERS manager.

CSAA's road service equipment started with two Alco touring cars that were converted to tow cars. The 1912 or 1913 Alcos had been built by the American Locomotive Co., and cost $6,000-$7,000 when new. They were used at seasonal tow camps near Yosemite.

The 9.5-liter, six-cylinder engine developed 60 hp. The CSAA service-car fleet was eventually expanded with the advent of regular emergency CSAA road services. Other early tow cars were also big, older, luxury cars converted to service trucks in the association's shop. One Locomobile used in emergency road service had begun its life, about 1920, as a hardtop touring car. It had a massive six-cylinder, 95-hp engine.

During the '20s, it cost about $1,800 to buy a suitable used car and convert it into a fully equipped tow car. CSAA official Clarke Cottrell researched ERS methods and equipment and recommended supplementing the tow cars with eight $600 Harley-Davidson motorcycles to use as service vehicles.

Cottrell's 1923 research into ERS methods and equipment showed: "The motorcycles of the Chicago Club are all Harley-Davidsons. The Chicago Club claims this is by far the best make and they selected this type of equipment after very unfortunate experience with lighter machines."

The rear view of the Lincoln CSAA service vehicle shows its famous tow dolly, used for cars of the era with solid axles. The Lincoln also has chromed rails and a spotlight. (John Gunnell)

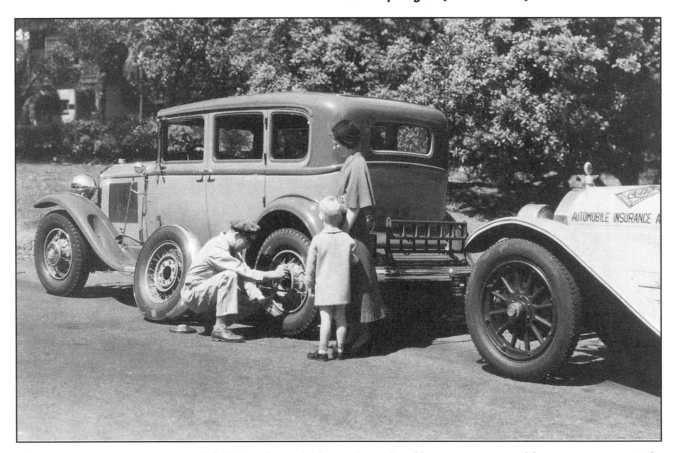

Members could depend on the CSAA for dependable road service. Here a woman and her young son watch a tire being changed on their sedan. (John Gunnell)

A September 1925 CSAA publication shows a CSAA attendant jacking a car. The tow dolly offered leverage to raise a car and allowed easy towing in the solid axle era. (John Gunnell)

CSAA campaigned for construction of a Victory Highway between San Francisco and New York. In 1926, it participated in Motorland magazine's "great motor caravan" from San Francisco to Salt Lake City, commemorating efforts to improve that section of the route and blaze the trail for a stream of motorists to come to California. CSAA also started using contract garages to do towing.

"The success of the contract garages is the success of the service," Cottrell said.

ERS expanded in the '20s, with members receiving service from association members and independently contracted gas stations. Cottrell always stressed the importance of getting the right kind of operators involved when contract service stations were chosen and he insisted that the club always should deal with them fairly.

"Extreme care should be used in selecting these garages," he wrote. "A spirit of good will and hearty co-operation will have to be engendered and maintained. Without that, success will be difficult."

In 1999, CSAA manager of field operations Jim LaCunha said, "What I learned from my predecessors is they selected (contract) stations on the basis of the quality and character of the people they contracted with and that's the way we still do it!"

Independent contract stations (ICS) handled 84 calls in the first month of ERS operation and reimbursements to them from CSAA amounted to $101.96 ($1.21 per call). By the next December, there were 171 contract stations that answered 1,062 monthly calls at a cost to the club of $1,603.76 ($1.51 per call).

From the beginning, ERS kept track of all calls. In the first few months, tire blowouts and ignition troubles were the biggest problems. The categories "stuck in sand," "stuck in mud" and "out of water" involved the fewest members.

A handsome hardcover book edited by Lynn Swanson and John Goepel and titled ERS: The Early Years was published in 1999 by Via Books (800) 999-4650 or (888) 577-4759. Website: www.tehabi.com.

This "accident" was arranged by the CSAA in 1937 at a San Francisco intersection. A tow truck backs to the damaged Cord sedan. The "victim" is definitely in character! (John Gunnell)

AUTOMOBILE ASSOCIATIONS OFFER A LITTLE HELP ALONG THE WAY *By Tom Collins*

In a remote Swiss mountain pass, on the crowded streets of Sao Paulo, Brazil, or in the oven-like outback of Australia, automobile club-sponsored assistance is ready to calm distressed drivers and keep their vehicles running.

Automobile clubs began at a time when roads were poor, vehicles often broke down and road maps were just being created. A heritage of service and assistance has been the result for decades.

Americans and Canadians are aware of their automobile associations—AAA and CAA. Both have existed since the early days of motoring.

One of the oldest groups in England is the AA (Automobile Association) which offers members uniformed patrols, trained repair personnel and no charges for roadside breakdowns. Another veteran British organization is the RAC (Royal Automobile Club) which includes horse trailer service among its offerings.

More than five million members trust the British service, Green Flag, which focuses on rapid assistance and customer care.

Regardless of where they're located, service organizations often are best identified by the person who drives the service vehicle and reaches out to people in need.

Here are a few of the world's auto service organizations:

—Allegemeiner Deutscher Automobil Club now serves more than 12 million members and has been in business since 1903 in Germany.

—The Australian Automobile Association has served the land down under since 1924.

—The Royal Automobile Club (RAC) also helps people in each Australian territory.

—CET (Companhia de Engenharia de Trafego) routes drivers in busy urban Brazil.

—Autoliito is the automotive association in Finland while Icelandic AA cares for people in that island nation.

—Japan Camping Association and Japan Automobile Federation offer tips for member travelers.

—Magyar Autoklub serves the needs of busy drivers in Hungary.

—Kiwi drivers enjoy help from the Automobile Association of New Zealand (AANZ).

—Polski Zwiazek Motorowy is the Polish Automobile and Motorcycle Federation serving members there.

—In Sweden, Svenska Turistforeningen and The M (Motormannens Riksforbund) are among the available automobile clubs.

—Among the services offered by the Automobile Association of Singapore are scrap car service, pre-trip inspection and road tax advice.

—The Touring Club Schweiz serves German, Italian and French speakers with separate sites in this multi-lingual nation.

—Indian associations include the Western India Automobile Association and the Automobile Association of Southern India.

—The Chinese Taipei Automobile Association can help drivers on the islands of Taiwan and Formosa.

Auto clubs, tow trucks and help all go together for busy motorists wherever they're from.

Green Flag
motoring assistance

CHAPTER 9
ON THE TRACK

LIFE IN THE PITS: TOW VEHICLES AT RACETRACKS

By Ron Kowalke

Auto racing is a sport filled with danger. Race cars competing at high speed within inches of each other produces excitement for the spectators in the grandstands or viewers watching on television, but it also poses a huge risk for drivers.

Wheels accidentally touch and cars skid out of control and smash into the cement walls or guard rails that line oval tracks. Worse, the contact sends a race car into a series of metal-crunching flips.

Once the crashing stops, spectators take a breath and watch vigilantly, hoping the drivers involved exit their wrecked cars and are able to walk away uninjured. Once the signal is given that all drivers involved are okay and clear of their cars, the next step is for the accident scene to be cleared. The most important vehicle to accomplish this task is the racetrack's tow truck.

Tow trucks have been a part of motor sports since its inception. They come in all sizes, and some can't even be categorized as a truck. Clearing the wreckage of race cars from accident scenes is a primary duty, but it's not the only duty track-side tow rigs perform.

Tow trucks come in handy for giving race cars a push start, a common practice at open wheel events featuring sprint cars or midgets. Inclement weather often mires race haulers in muddy pit area surfaces and they need a tow to higher or drier ground.

Tow trucks also play a ceremonial role, acting as race event flag bearers or chauffeuring racers around the track during introductions. A tow truck also helps when a driver who has been black flagged for improper conduct decides to protest by parking on the track.

This type of tow duty illustrates the phrase: "Getting the hook!"

Race track tow duties can be prestigious as well as serious duty. Some of the most visible tow trucks can be found each Memorial Day weekend glistening in the spotlight of one of motor sports most hallowed events, the Indianapolis 500.

*A former military vehicle, this **McGinty Auto Sales** tow truck rolls into action at the hallowed "Brickyard" in 1947. (Indianapolis Motor Speedway)*

This 1981 GMC Sierra Grande 3/4 ton was ready for race day from its clean push bumper and grille guard to its rear mud flaps. It carries a very sleek Holmes tow unit. (Indianapolis Motor Speedway)

In 1988, the official tow truck of the 72nd Indianapolis 500 was built on an '88 GMC Sierra Grande chassis and carried a Challenger tow unit. (Indianapolis Motor Speedway)

The Gilmore Lion Head Special 2 Big Car is readied for towing after a dirt track tumble. Note the dapper appearance of the tow truck driver (left) and track official (right). (Bruce Craig)

CHAPTER 10
COLLECTORS

EVERY TOWER NEEDS A HOBBY—LIKE OLD CARS

By John Gunnell

"You have to take every day as a gift," says towing service operator Todd Klismet, of Waupaca, Wis. "Instead of taking things too seriously all of the time, you have to take time to enjoy yourself, too." Todd, who runs the service department at Waupaca Mobil Travel Center, collects old cars. He feels that his owning and restoring a 1964 Ford Galaxie and 1971 Pontiac LeMans have increased both his family fun and his customer satisfaction level.

Todd, his wife Faye and his daughters Kelsey, 4, and Alexis, 8, attend four to five old car shows per year and go to weekly "cruise-ins" at the local Burger King on summer nights. "I really enjoy going to the cruises with the kids," Todd told me. "Just driving there and back makes for some very enjoyable family time." The Klismets also take part in a fall color car cruise in which the old car group travels through the autumn countryside for several hours.

The lessons Todd learned through getting his old cars in pristine condition and maintaining them through the seasons have also contributed to the way that he runs his profession. "From collecting cars, I know how to take care of cars," he points out. "For instance, I put leather gloves over the J-hooks so I don't scratch the paint on a car's axle. I also think more about where I place the hooks, because there's only so many spots where you can safely hook up."

Being a car enthusiast helps Todd sympathize with folks when they get uptight about their favorite car being towed. "I tell them that I'm a car collector and it absolutely does help them feel more relaxed about their problem," he says.

Todd Klismet poses with his 1971 Pontiac Le Mans 400 two-door hardtop and one of the two wheel-lift trucks he operates. The WMTC fleet also includes a flatbed and a tire service truck. (John Gunnell)

Some of the rare cars that Klismet has towed include a very nice 1973 Jaguar XKE that the owner wanted to transport to a shop for service, a limited-edition Callaway Twin-Turbo Corvette that lost its clutch, a Plymouth 440-powered Road Runner and a Stage 1 Buick muscle car.

Todd says that he's been collecting cars since an early age. Cars were always one of his strongest interests. He purchased his 1971 LeMans 400 hardtop when he was 17 years old and in high school. He has also owned several old Thunderbirds. He did mechanical work on a 1950 Ford Tudor that his father had owned since 1971.

It was Todd's father who purchased Waupaca Mobil Travel Center five years after purchasing that old Ford. He later took over the car repair shop and the family entered the towing business in 1980. Today there are seven employees and four trucks: two wheel-lift units, one flatbed and one tire service truck. Brand-wise, the trucks include an older IH, two Chevys and a Ford. "The equipment today is so much better than what we used years ago," says Todd. "I think a flatbed is the safest way to haul, because once the car is on a flatbed, you have full control."

Although Wisconsin's icy winter roads are a challenge to drivers, Todd's busiest month is usually in the heart of the old-car show season and can cut a bit into his hobby hours at times. "Summer is the tourist season," he explains. "July is probably still the largest month, but if it's real, real cold, January can be the biggest."

Klismet focuses on number of calls as an important factor in running his operation profitably. "For us, money is made in volume, rather than investing in big equipment; a day with lots of tows is a good day. On that kind of day you get cars in a ditch, people skidding off the road and it's typically a weather-driven type of thing that's hard to schedule for. They keep you going." Todd's brother Steve keeps a scrapbook of photos showing the jobs handled over the years. They range from towing a restored MG to water recoveries from the lakes around the area.

While Klismet feels that his hobby helps him run his business better, sometimes a towing job can contribute to his hobby enjoyment. "The things you find in people's barns and garages are amazing; nice, older cars that don't get out much," Todd advises. "We towed a 1971 Lincoln that had only 9,000 miles on it and I found a really nice, rust-free parts car from Texas that was a four-door, but had some very nice parts that I wanted for my two-door hardtop." He adds, "If people know you're interested in old cars, they'll say, 'let me show you something.'"

Part of Todd's enthusiasm for classic cars and his love of the towing industry is reflected in an event called "Trucker's Pride" that takes place at Waupaca Mobil Travel Center every fall. It attracts all kinds of trucks from all over the country and includes a judging class for tow trucks.

When asked if he ever thinks about restoring an older tow truck to add to his collection and display at Trucker's Pride, Todd says "I haven't given that much consideration, but I did tow one once. A big collector with over 20 early-'50s IH trucks purchased it from a town near here and had us tow it to his collection."

Todd says telling his customers he's a car collector "absolutely does help" them feel better about having their favorite car towed. (John Gunnell)

A WOMAN'S HOME IS HER TOY TOW TRUCK MUSEUM

By John Gunnell

A man's home may be his castle, but a woman's home is her tow truck museum . . . at least if Betty Parnham's house in Stevens Point, Wisconsin, is any indication. Betty says she has "...more than 500 and probably 800..." miniature tow trucks scattered throughout her one-story home. In addition, she has lined the walls with tow truck art.

Tow truck memorabilia decorates every nook and cranny between the kitchen and her son's bedroom.

Betty's husband, Darrell, has been involved in the towing industry since 1980 and gained notoriety for risking his life during one emergency. Darrell's life was different before the couple met.

"Darrell was devoted to the towing business 24 hours a day and had no social life."

Darrell actually had towed Betty's car several times, but it wasn't until they met at a bonfire that their courtship began. They were engaged within three months and married a year and a half later.

Darrell worked for Bob "Hawkeye" Johnson of Amherst, Wisconsin. Bob played an important part in helping Darrell and Betty take over Johnson Towing, of Stevens Point, which they now operate together. Johnson, who still operates Johnson's Towing of Amherst, Inc., gave the couple up-front, honest answers about the business and still helps them with paperwork and advice. Betty also credits the trade publication *Footnotes Towing & Recovery News* with helping get the business off the ground.

"I was really motivated by an article that told you to have 'all your ducks in a row' before you go to the bank for a business loan."

This brown wooden toy with "Johnson 24 Hour Towing" on its sides was the first miniature tow truck in Betty Parnham's collection. (John Gunnell)

Betty Parnham of Johnson Towing, Stevens Point, poses with just a portion of her 800-piece "private museum" collection of towing industry memorabilia. (John Gunnell)

After seeing this Danbury Mint model featured in Footnotes, Betty not only bought the vehicle, she tracked down the publicity photo framed behind the Chevrolet miniature. (John Gunnell)

Betty started collecting miniature tow trucks three years ago. The first one she got was a large wooden replica crafted by a friend.

"Now I can't go to Wal-Mart or K-Mart without looking for tow trucks in the toy aisle," she says with a laugh.

Betty enjoys focusing on the small details of each model.

"I like things that are different and unique so I can sit on the floor with them and look at all the little features," she says. "I'm really intrigued with such miniatures as

Danbury Mint models, because everything works."

From miniature tow trucks, Betty's collection has boomed to include sweaters, baby outfits, art prints, pedal cars, glasses, magnets, bottle openers, shirts, sweatshirts, blankets, greeting cards, cookie cutters and tow-truck Christmas presents.

After seeing an article about a Danbury Mint tow truck in *Footnotes*, Betty bought the replica and then tracked down the writer to buy the color publicity photo of the toy that appeared in the magazine! Her devotion to making the

Betty loves small details and often collects similar models with different color schemes and lettering. Several examples are included in this custom-built case. (John Gunnell)

collection complete and interesting seems to know no bounds.

Betty also enjoys showing off her collection in ways that promote the towing industry. Two years ago, she had some of the toy tow trucks on display at the Stevens Point Mall. She also filled a glass display case at the local library with miniature haulers.

"The librarian told me the kids liked the tow truck display the best," she recalls.

Darrell says, "Betty is a good promoter and does a great job promoting our business."

Betty also is active in the Wisconsin Towing Association and donated a pedal car tow truck that brought a nice price in the WTA's annual auction. Her attention to detail showed when she placed a "tow bear" with a set of jumper cables in the seat of the toy car.

In addition to buying toys at local department stores and from mail-order houses, Betty visits old-car swap meets. She's also up-to-speed on using the Internet to track down tiny towers that can't be found in other places.

"I bought two boxes of broken toy tow trucks on eBay," she advises.

While collecting toys and models makes work fun, it also contributes to the actual operation of Johnson Towing, since Betty puts a lot of emphasis on small details and business-promoting activities. She is very picky about running clean trucks.

"The appearance of both your toy trucks and real trucks comes across as your image."

Betty's business promotion seems to come naturally and isn't just publicity hype. Darrell related the story of a woman with small kids breaking down.

"Betty brought them to the house, fed them and gave the kids toy tow trucks," he recalls.

Her energy for the industry and positive attitude also make Betty a great bill collector, her husband says.

"You've got to love what you're doing and I do," Betty chimes in.

"I think that the towing industry has been on the back burner too long, but it's a profession," says Betty. "You have to like it and you have to enjoy what you're doing – you just have to be a people person."

Betty even has a tow truck-shaped weather vane in her collection. (John Gunnell)

Betty Parnham's attention to detail spills over to the real Johnson Towing trucks, which she insists be clean and attractively painted. (John Gunnell)

FASCINATED BY TOW TRUCK PHOTOS

By John Gunnell

"I have always been fascinated by tow trucks—and what a necessary workhorse they have proven to be," says Coy Thomas, the owner of Coy's Reliable Auto Parts in Port Angeles, Washington.

In addition to supplying parts to antique car collectors, Thomas is a collector of cars, trucks and automobilia. He always enjoys sharing his acquisitions with others who are interested in vintage vehicles and their history.

After Coy sent several outstanding tow truck photos to Krause Publications, we discovered there was no common theme we could use to weave a story. We asked Thomas to try to explain his fascination with tow trucks and to give his thoughts and reflections on the old tow truck photos he'd sent us.

According to Coy, part of his fascination with tow truck photos stems from what he sees as the tow truck's most important role – helping folks in a jam.

"Many people have found themselves stranded or in dire need of removing their car from a dangerous situation," he notes.

"A tow truck always comes speeding to the rescue, ready to help out, even if the problem is relatively minor, like a flat tire or a dead battery."

Through collecting old photos at garage sales, swap meets and car shows, Thomas has formed his own, informal views about the development of the towing industry.

"By reviewing old photos, you can readily see that large antique or classic cars were pressed into service as towing rigs way before the vehicle-recovery industry progressed to specialty trucks," Thomas advises.

"These big automobiles of the past, including classic Cadillacs and Packards, had the weight and horsepower that was required to remove smaller, more economical cars from accident scenes and roadside ditches."

According to Thomas, the big classic cars also had the ability to keep up with the era's highway speeds, even while pulling a damaged or broken car to what he calls a "holding" yard.

This Chevrolet carried the name of Morrison Motors Limited of Duncan, British Columbia. Morrison Motors was a "GM Factory Approved Body and Fender Repairs" facility that offered "24 Hour Towing Service." (Coy Thomas Photo Collection)

Rollovers presented a challenge for any tow truck, such as this rig that ran out of Globe, Arizona. Instead of advertising "24-hour service," the slogan on the door gave the phone number "100" and said to call "Any Time." (Coy Thomas Photo Collection)

These locations sometimes were the next-to-last stop for such vehicles.

"Usually, back in the '20s or '30s, the tow service operator also had an adjoining salvage yard," Coy recalls. "They often had the insurance claim or customers wanting parts off the damaged cars. Many cars were acquired by such salvage yards simply in exchange for towing fees that the owners couldn't or wouldn't pay."

From studying his old photos, Thomas believes that as tow trucks — both homemade and commercially-built versions — became more common, the mechanics who ran them found it necessary to have such a rig at their disposal for picking up future repair jobs or for re-doing a completed job that had gone bad.

"Transmission shops always had their share of these workhorses," Coy emphasizes.

"This was particularly the case after the introduction of the automatic transmission, with its unpredictable bands or 'lock-ups.' It was hard for a car to 'limp' home with a bum automatic transmission."

One thing that Coy Thomas finds especially fascinating when it comes to old tow truck photos is scenes showing the trucks responding to vehicle rollovers.

"The pictures show that many rollovers required a husky tow truck, with lots of cable, to winch the rolled vehicle back up a hillside inch by inch," he explains. "Sometimes, two tow trucks were needed, so that one could anchor onto the other one." Coy adds that larger tow trucks became a necessity as cars increased in size.

There are interesting stories behind many pictures of vintage tow trucks. Coy Thomas has learned the same thing through collecting such photos.

He points to a photo of an early-'50s Chevy tow truck operated by a Canadian car dealer as one example. This truck carried the name of Morrison Motors on its door, along with the frequently-seen "24 HR. Towing SERVICE" advertisement.

The Chevy had the two-digit phone number "30" lettered on the sides of the body and identified Morrison Motors as a "GM Factory Approved Body and Fender Repairs" facility.

"Many dealers, such as Newell Morrison, of Duncan, British Columbia, needed a dependable tow truck to take care of customer needs," says Thomas. "The dealerships were usually encouraged, by the Big Three automakers that franchised them, to have a complete service shop that offered everything from repairs to towing."

Coy notes that his collection indicates that other roadside service groups – such as the Automobile Club of America or AAA – helped make needed tow truck service more convenient for their members.

"Their trucks also served as a 'sales pitch' for their organization," Thomas adds. "The oval-shaped AAA symbol became synonymous with roadside assistance in the very early days of highway travel."

In addition to collecting old tow truck photos, Coy Thomas sometimes goes to car shows and takes his own photos of restored tow trucks. These have included a Model AA Ford roadster pickup built by F & M Towing of San Jose, California, and an orange 1935 Ford hot rod. He spotted both at the Hot August Nights show in Reno, Nevada in the summer of 2002.

"As the years have gone by, many tow truck lovers have located vintage trucks that needed to be updated," says Thomas. "They add lots of chrome plating, possibly a modern engine and often use their rigs to advertise a past or current business, thereby keeping the interest in older tow trucks alive."

TOW VETERAN ENJOYS GOING "TOPLESS"

By Tom Collins

Some tow truck operators become attached to cars they rescue. Henry Vanden Heuvel of Kaukauna, Wisconsin, began a long-term collecting hobby when he rescued and repaired a damaged '63 Corvair.

"It ran over a mailbox attached to a block of concrete," he says. "The concrete tore into the engine and the oil pan. It was a fun little car—but not very practical for my wife and six kids!"

Henry sold that Corvair but bought a '64 model and began to build his collection. Now he has five Corvair convertibles.

"Someone told me convertibles were more valuable—and they're a lot more fun, too!"

He worked for auto body shops from the time he was 21 until 1955 when he opened Henry's Auto Body on the busy Highway 96 borderline of Little Chute and Kaukauna.

Little Chute village police chief Robert Nechodem convinced Henry he needed to add a towing service. Eventually, the business became Henry's Inc.

"I built my first wrecker in 1955," he says. "We had 19 trucks through the years including Whites, Internationals, and GMCs."

One of his early tow vehicles was a Jeep FC 170. He fondly remembers his last two trucks from the 1970s.

"That White was a nice one and the GMC had a 10-speed Road Ranger."

Today, Henry's "topless" collection also includes a 1963 Thunderbird convertible in addition to his Corvairs. The Thunderbird was another "rescue" project.

"The owner was losing his eyesight and wanted me to look at it. I thought it was dandy."

Henry says it's fun driving one of his convertibles. Often, one or more of his six children or special friend, Diane Niemuth, drive them in parades. Henry also enjoys going to car shows or Corvair club events. And you'll often see him just taking a ride, with the top down whenever possible.

"I bought them over a number of years. They're my fun cars."

In 1972, Henry survived a head on collision while driving a tow truck. He still has pain from that accident but feels lucky because the driver of the car that hit him died instantly. In the late '70s, Henry lost his partner and ace radio person, his wife, Kathleen. Soon he retired from towing to work on his cars and cherish his vivid memories.

"I thought of writing a book called *Looking Through the Windshield of a Tow Truck.*," he says. "We helped a lot of people get out who were pinned in cars over the years."

If you're in the Little Chute or Kaukauna areas of northeast Wisconsin, you might see Henry in one of his "topless" cars. Be sure to smile at the driver.

Henry Vanden Heuvel goes "topless" in his Corvairs for parades and car shows. He has red, white and blue versions. (Henry Vanden Heuvel)

At one point, Henry's collection also included a Cadillac convertible but he sold it. He still has the Thunderbird and is very active in Corvair clubs. (Henry Vanden Heuvel)

CHAPTER 11
TOY TOW TRUCKS

SMALL NODS TO THE PAST

By John Gunnell

Some people form a desire to own an old tow truck after reading about towing history in collector magazines like *Old Cars Weekly* or in trade publications like *Footnotes Towing and Recovery News*. Often they figure they can buy an antique truck, paint it up in their company colors and write it off as a promotional item.

This can be done if handled in the right manner but the job of properly restoring any vehicle (and particularly a hardworking, well-used tow truck) can eat up oodles of money. For many operators, the best alternative to restoring a full-sized truck might be buying a small one.

Toy and model companies like First Gear, Ertl and Maisto offer a number of different tow truck models. One is based on a '49 Ford pickup, another is a '37 Chevy 1-1/2-ton and another is a big '57 IHC. A firm called On Mark International is among several companies that will cus-

tomize the pint-size classics to your liking.

You can have one of the available models finished to match your modern tow trucks and have it decorated with decals that duplicate your company's name, logo or slogan. The model can then be used for everything from holiday gift giving to an incentive for your employees to do an outstanding job. Some of the trucks can even be sold to people who collect branded collectibles. If your color scheme and decorations prove popular, the sales to collectors may even pay for the "whole shooting match."

On Mark International and similar companies buy the models in quantity and imprint the logos and other customizing touches for companies large and small. Different versions of the 1949 Ford tow truck made by Maisto have been decorated with the logos of several major petroleum retailers including Texaco, Shamrock, Cities Service,

Many of today's tow truck drivers and enthusiasts probably grew up with a toy tow truck like this one in their collections. Now it would be considered a collectible. (Ron Kowalke)

Many of today's tow truck drivers probably grew up with a toy tow truck like this one. Now it would be considered a collectible. (Ron Kowalke)

Shell licensed On Mark International to do the '37 Chevy tow truck with a striped bumper. (On Mark International)

Mobilgas and Phillips 66.

A model of a 1937 Chevy 1-1/2-ton tow truck made by First Gear has also been produced with Shell and Texaco decals.

Not all of On Mark International's customers are large companies, however. The firm, which is headquartered in Oklahoma, also did a beautiful job of customizing Ertl's 1/34th-scale model of a 1957 International tow truck for Storey Wrecker Services, Inc., which has locations in Broken Arrow and Tulsa, Oklahoma.

The imprinted models mate the appreciation many people who've worked on tow trucks have for them with the respect the public has for towing services. After all, many people have had to call tow trucks to come to their rescue after breaking down on the road.

On Mark International also sells the excess inventory from some jobs it has done in the past by mail order and via the Internet. You can contact them at (918) 446-7906 or visit their online catalog at www.onmarkint.com.

The popularity of real Ford wreckers hasn't been lost on toy manufacturers. This 1949 Ford F-1 pickup with towing crane is one of the miniatures available. Both Texaco and Phillips logos were available. (OCW)

This detailed "Advanced Design" Chevrolet 3800 wrecker was offered by the Danbury Mint. (OCW)

The 1937 Chevy tow truck model is designed to promote Texaco products and service. (On Mark International)

SMITH MILLER WRECKERS

By John Gunnell

Do you know the difference between a toy tow truck and a model of one? To a collector a toy tow truck is a miniature version of the real thing. A model is a miniature of a real tow truck built to a specific scale.

A toy version may resemble a specific tow truck or may be "generic." One toy may look like a Ford, although its proportions have actually been "eyeballed" by a toymaker, rather than measured by a modeler. Another toy may be made by Fisher-Price for small kids and look nothing like a real truck.

A model would be an accurate miniature of a certain real tow truck manufactured to scale. For example, there's a miniature tow truck that Mobil Oil released as a promotional item. The blue plastic model looks exactly like a 1988 Chevy scaled down to "table-top" size. Most models come in popular scales such as 1/10th (one inch on the model equals 10 inches on the real truck), 1/24th, 1/25th and 1/32nd, but a model can also have its own unique scale.

This chapter focuses on the outstanding "toy" wreckers made by the "modern" Smith-Miller Company, founded by Fred Thompson and operated by his son.

All Smith-Miller tow trucks are really toys, although they are very close to being models. Shown with this column is the Howard Sommers Tow Truck with Sleeper. This large toy was released in 1998. It measures approximately 24-1/2 inches overall and is constructed of steel and aluminum with rubber tires.

Smith-Miller started making high-quality toys right after World War II. The company closed in the mid-'50s. By 1979, the toys were becoming serious collectibles. One collector named Fred Thompson tracked down the firm's former owner while he was chasing after parts to fix an original. Thompson – who lived in Los Angeles then — discovered that the company's parts inventory still existed in Santa Monica, Calif., and he managed to buy it. Since then, he has issued 23 new Smith-Miller toys with the looks, quality and collectibility of the old ones.

The Smith-Miller "L" series Mack tow truck was built in a limited edition of 250 copies. (Smith Miller)

The Howard Sommers tow truck is the fourth Smith-Miller wrecker. The first wrecker came out in 1987. It was based on the 1940s-style Mack Model B truck cab. This toy was issued in a bright red Los Angeles Fire Dept. version as well as civilian versions that carried "Smitty Toys" decals and came in solid orange, yellow-and-blue and black-and-gold color selections. Thompson made 125 copies of each version.

In 1994, Thompson released two additional tow trucks, both based on the early-'50s style Mack Model L. The first toy (250 made) came in orange-and-blue with "Smitty's Garage"and "Union 76" decals. The second version of the toy featured the same basic configuration and 225 were made. The latter edition was painted black-and-white and had a red emergency light on the cab. It was decorated with "Black & White Garage" and "L.A.P.D." decals

The Howard Sommers wrecker was issued in 1998. The solid red super-duty tow truck was the first Smith-Miller

tow truck with a sleeper and the first to have exhaust stacks, running lights and a horn. It has what is called the "M.I.C." style cab (Miller-Ironson Corp. –or M.I.C.—was the original company's final trade name) with mid-1950s Styling. The M.I.C. toy also resembles a Mack, but it does not carry Mack's "bulldog" emblem.

All of the Smith-Miller wreckers are designed for collectors and are priced accordingly. The Howard Sommers version is still available right from Thompson's new headquarters in Arizona and carries a price tag of $1,095!

To find out more contact: Smith-Miller, 68 Mulberry Ave., Lake Havasu City, AZ 86403 or call Fred Thompson at (818) 703-8588. You can also visit www.smith-miller.com on the Internet.

AN "IDEAL" TOW TRUCK INVESTMENT

By John Gunnell

Like many tow truck enthusiasts, you probably never fail to give in to the allure of a miniature tow truck—whether the miniature is a toy, a model, a whiskey decanter or a ceramic sculpture. As soon as you see it, there's a good chance you'll want to add it to your collection—if the price is reasonable.

During the past year or two, there seems to be even more motivation for investing in such miniatures. Please note the use of the word "investing."

If you put $200 in a stock market portfolio or mutual fund in the past year or two, you probably still have $120 left, if you're lucky. If you bought a $200 antique toy at the same time, you still have a $200 antique toy. Maybe it's worth $250, $300 or even $400!

There's no guarantee you made money on the old toy, but you probably didn't lose any money either. That's one reason serious investors move out of equities and into "hard" assets when the economy tightens up. Collectibles are a good place to park your money for a while and toys and models are a pretty safe bet to hold or increase their value.

Also, toys are fairly durable items—at least the old-fashioned ones. Stamps can tear, coins are easily lost and antique cars need maintenance.

On the other hand, old toys are sturdy and if they need some paint touch-up or minor repair, it's usually not a big deal, nor too big of an expense, to restore them.

Most toy collectors tend to collect the toys they had or wanted to have when they were kids. Possibly, you went through that phase between the late 1940s and late 1950s. When girls came along, toys no longer seemed important. During that period, some great toys were made by an outfit called Ideal Toy Co.

Ideal was a New Jersey toy maker active in the postwar period. The company was known for a wide variety of products in many different categories.

Perhaps you remember their plastic Roy Rogers stagecoach, their talking Robert the Robot and their nearly life-size Patti Playpal doll.

Ideal later merged with Sawyer's ViewMaster. The company was ultimately taken over by Tyco Toy Co. Tyco was then consumed by Mattel.

The Ideal name no longer is used, but during the '50s, it was found on many plastic toy cars and trucks, including several types of tow trucks known as "Fix-It" and "Motorific." In the 1960s, the company shortened its name to ITC. Some of the same toys, as well as some new ones, were produced under the ITC brand.

Many of the Ideal and ITC vehicles were large-scale replicas of actual cars and trucks cast in colorful heavy plastic and designed to be put together fully or partially with screws.

There was a huge '53 Corvette with fabric that glued to the seats and large reproductions of a number of famous imported cars of the early postwar era including a Ferrari, an MG TD, a Jaguar XK-140 coupe and a Mercedes-Benz 300 convertible sedan. Some later ITC models are glue-together kits with smaller dimensions.

Toy tow trucks were made in several different versions in both the '50s and '60s, but the most collectible one probably is the streamlined "Ideal Fix-It Tow Truck" produced in the company's early years. It seems to be based on a toy open-cab fire engine and it is apparently very hard to find today.

According to a 1997 book called the *Toy Cars & Trucks Identification and Value Guide, 2nd Edition*, by Richard O'Brien, this Ideal Toy was considered so rare the collector value for an in-the-box example cannot be estimated. Collectors consider toys that are still in their original box to be worth premium prices.

Like many Ideal toys, this Fix-It truck was designed so a child could take it apart and put it back together. It came with a tool box and toy tools to help with assembly and included a toy 1951 Chevrolet with a dented fender.

A picture of the truck is shown on page 239 of the book and the text notes: "Ideal Fix-It Tow Truck and Car with fender. 20-1/2-inch plastic and metal truck holds tools for chaining tires and fender. Also has battery-operated searchlight, crank-operated tow crane and fire extinguisher, $9.95."

The book estimates the toy truck by itself, without the damaged Chevrolet or the box, can be valued at $90-$180 in toy grading conditions C6 to C10. Condition C6 is described as "well played with, but still collectible" and condition C10 is "mint."

One of these toy tow trucks showed up recently on eBay, the international online auction site. It included the original box and assembly instructions – both in mint condition – as well as the truck and the damaged Chevrolet.

The seller said that, to the best of his knowledge, only a few small pieces were missing from the 50-plus-year-old toy. They included the front bumper of the car, plus the bolt and nut to assemble the front bumper to the car, the lens assembly that holds the light in the spotlight and the fire extinguisher that sits on the corner of the tow truck's front bumper.

All of the other parts on the truck and car were in

"played-with-but-not-damaged" condition. The seller noted the toy jack even ratcheted up to lift the truck or car and that the wheels of the truck were removable with the toy wrenches.

A $200 reserve price was placed on this collectible toy tow truck. When the auction was over, it had been bid to only $139.06 and it did not sell. It may still be in Cranberry Township, Pennsylvania, looking for a new and young-at-heart owner.

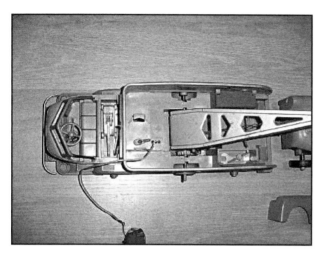

The "Ideal Fix-it-Tow Truck" had an open top and an operating tow crane. (John Gunnell)

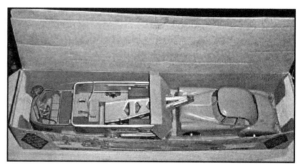

The "Ideal Fix-It-Tow Truck" had an open top, operating tow crane and pulled a 1950 Chevrolet. (John Gunnell)

COLLECTING TOW TOYS = FAMILY FUN

By John Gunnell

The necessity of planning some "family time" seems to be of major concern to towing professionals. Something that any family involved in the towing industry can do together is collect toy tow trucks and tow-truck models.

Do you know the difference between a "toy" and a "model?" Technically, a toy is a replica of the real thing and a model is a replica of the real thing built to a particular scale.

Toy tow trucks may be slightly more interesting because a toy maker can suspend reality to create his or her own great design. The model maker is locked into very accurately recreating someone else's design. With a 1:12-scale model, for instance, each inch of the model would be an exact copy of each foot of the real tow truck.

For collectors, both toys and models can be separated into different categories. Antique toys or models would be those made many years ago, as opposed to a replica of an old tow truck manufactured last year. There are also toys that look like the real item (though they may not be done to scale) like a Tonka tow truck. These are much more realistic than a Fisher-Price tow truck made for a two-year-old.

A serious toy or model collector might specialize in collecting one type or brand of miniature tow trucks, but a tow truck professional who collects as a hobby is much more likely to have a diverse collection--anything as long as it's a tow truck. And the serious collector may want every toy stored in its original box, as opposed to the tow-ing professional, who's more inclined to display his or her collection over the fireplace.

If you become a casual collector and get your family involved in your hobby, you can have lots of fun scouting for your next acquisition. You'll find your kids dragging you to the toy department the next time you stop at Wal-Mart and your significant other will be looking for little tow trucks as he or she peruses the treasures at the local antique shop.

To find out how easy it is to hunt for old toy tow trucks, we paid a visit to the antique emporium in our little village. Only 1,000 souls live in Iola, Wis., but there is a new antique shop that had three old tow truck toys for sale. Strangely enough, the prices quoted by proprietor Duke Tuomi ran inversely to the size of the toys. A large Nylint truck from the '70s or '80s could be had for $25, an in-the-middle-sized Hubley truck from the '40s or '50s was tagged

$89.95 and a smaller Hubley from about the same era had a $95 asking price.

Of course, these days it's not even necessary to visit an antique shop to look for older tow truck toys and models. The world's inventory is at your fingertips if you have a computer and an eBay account. The online auction not only has a great selection of such items for sale, but some great values as well. That's because the competition is keen and the marketplace is the entire world.

If you want to make collecting toy tow trucks a family hobby, the trick is to let other family members get just as involved as you are. If you wind up surfing the Web all night, instead of helping the kids with their homework, the whole plan may backfire on you.

As you can tell by some of the prices quoted in this chapter, collecting toys and models can be expensive. However, the collector values of old toys seem to increase steadily. So the money you spend making purchases and acquiring new miniatures is likely to become a long-term investment.

Experts say that collecting one type of toy is a good way to build a valuable collection because it's easier to sell a "themed" collection if the need ever arises. If you do start building up a nice fleet of miniature tow trucks, be sure to keep a list of each piece you buy. It's easier to list them one by one than to start a list after you've purchased 100 items. And the list will come in handy for trading and insurance

This Hubley No. 474 Kiddie Toy tow truck, dating from the late 1940s or early 1950s, was found in a small-town antique shop. (John Gunnell)

purposes.

Hubley Toy Company's No. 452 Kiddie Toy tow truck was a bit smaller and was probably issued later than the No. 474 toy truck. (John Gunnell)

The Nylint toy company of Rockford, Illinois, used Ford emblems on this Classic toy known as
the Nylint Auto Repair 24 Hour Towing truck. (John Gunnell)

CHAPTER 12
THE UNUSUAL

CHEETAH: THE 100 MPH TOW TRUCK

By Tom Collins

Cheetah was the name of an unusual piggy-back tow truck that was designed and built by two hot rodders back in the '60s. The streamlined "tow trucks" were copies of sleekly-styled transporters that the Mercedes-Benz factory racing team used to haul its 300SL competition roadsters to Grand Prix races in the mid 1950s.

The Mercedes transporters appeared in 1954, causing a stir at race tracks around the world. They were styled to complement the sculptured sheet metal of the 300SLs. The automaker spent a pretty "Pfennig" to build them, but it paid off when enthusiast magazines gave "ink" to them.

Norm Holikamp and Don Allen read about the German trucks and decided they could construct a similar vehicle at a much lower cost. Their Cheetah mated the cab of a '59 Chevrolet El Camino pickup with the running gear of a Mercedes-Benz 300-S sedan.

The El Camino cab was bobbed off at the cowl line to eliminate the hood, fenders and other front sheet metal. Everything else, including the "dog-leg" windshield and wraparound rear window were blended into the rear of the Cheetah's custom fiberglass body. The rear end was stretched to keep the Cheetah from being too nose heavy. It had a short wheelbase and large front and rear overhangs.

The "gull-wing" '59 Chevrolet taillights blended nicely into the rear of the fiberglass body. Up front, four head-lamps were molded into the grille-less nose. Large air scoops were mounted on the sides of the body, just above the front wheel wells (actually near the center of the body).

Cheetahs incorporated a ramp-type loading mechanism. Owner/ restorer James M. Degnan supplied these photos of his Cheetah. (James Degnan)

The Cheetah needed them to duct cold air to its 300-cid Chevrolet engine, which was mounted behind the front wheels. Holikamp and Allen claimed that the big-block V-8 could propel the Cheetah to over 100 miles per hour with a racecar strapped on its back.

The two men planned to produce Cheetahs on a limited basis at $16,000 a pop. The publicity brought some inquiries, but only a few were sold. Dean Moon, a racing-equipment maker and father of "Baby Moon" hubcaps owned a Cheetah. Race driver Jack McAfee used one to carry his F-Junior Lotus racecar to a race in Domora, Calif., in 1960.

The Cheetah was based on the sleek 1954 Mercedes-Benz transporter. (OCW)

The Mercedes-Benz factory racing team used the transporters to haul its 300SL competition roadsters to Grand Prix races in the mid 1950s. (OCW)

Dean Moon's Cheetah now belongs to race-car buff James M. Degnan, who purchased it from Moon's widow. Degnan's Cheetah carries his Lotus 51 and Allard K-2 to vintage racing events. (James Degnan)

The Rhino: Piecing Together All The Leftovers *By Tom Collins*

The history of tow vehicles runs the gamut from custom super-sized trucks matched to brand new tow bodies to old pickups with angle-iron booms attached and a cable or chain for pulling.

Historically, tow operators have been very resourceful with used equipment or have fabricated their own tools and towing units.

Lincoln-Zephyr owner John Hanson of Boscawen, New Hampshire, had some leftover pieces and decided to build his own tow vehicle. He took a 1930s era AA Ford truck frame and inserted a 1940 Lincoln V-12 engine. He mounted a Manley hand-cranked tow arm on the back. On the dash is a working electric wall clock!

John has lifted a 1964 Dodge with his hard-working "Rhino." It shows what can be done with leftovers.

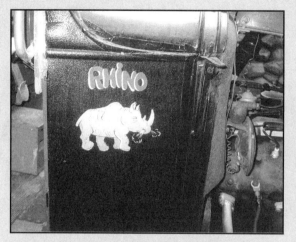

The "leftovers" tow truck with the big Lincoln V-12 is affectionately known as "Rhino." (John W. Hanson)

John Hanson of Boscawen, New Hampshire, used spare parts and a Lincoln Zephyr V-12 engine to build his own tow truck. (John W. Hanson)

ODDITIES

There's nothing like the tow truck fishing derby. Wonder what kind of line they're using on their tow booms? (Henry Vanden Heuvel)

The battery turned over—and so did the 1950 Chevy Deluxe two-door sedan! (Hap Cramer)

Looks like King Kong tried to install a sun roof in this 1963 Corvair. It's suffering a severe case of the "bends." (Hap Cramer)

There are squashed bugs on windshields. Here's a squashed "potato bug" Porsche on the back of this 1961 Chevy tow truck. (Hap Cramer)

It's the morning stretch at the tow truck garage. Breath in. Lift. Now how it...hold it... (Jay Lorenz)

CHAPTER 13
PRESERVED
AND
RESTORED

TOW TRUCK MUSEUM

By John Gunnell

If you love old-fashioned tow trucks and wreckers and you're making plans to be anywhere near Chattanooga, Tennessee, on a vacation or business trip, the International Towing and Recovery Hall of Fame is a place that you'll want to see. This unique little museum exhibits cars and trucks carrying wreckers and assorted towing equipment dating as far back as 1916. Also on exhibition are photos depicting early wreckers and the men who used them, as well as different toys and models of historical tow trucks.

Chattanooga was selected as the location for this museum because the city claims to be the place where the first wrecker was built 83 years ago. It was made by the Ernest Holmes Company in a factory that is just one block away from the current museum.

The museum's collection includes early wrecker equipment built by Holmes, Manley, Weaver and others. This equipment is mounted on a variety of automobile and truck chassis.

Whealon Towing and Service, Fond du Lac, Wisconsin, loaned the museum its red and white Chevrolet tow truck that carries a large Holmes 460 wrecker and 540-cradle combination. (International Towing and Recovery Museum)

An interesting combination is a late-1920s Holmes 485 wrecker mounted on a Locomobile coupe. This vehicle was donated to the museum by Bob Meyer's Towing & Recovery of Owensville, Ohio. It characterizes an era in which larger, powerful automobiles that had little used-car value after a couple of years, frequently were converted into "service cars" with towing booms and cranes.

The museum also features a Manley crane from the same period mounted on a '26 Model TT Ford truck. This unit came from Scotty's Carriage Works, of Cameron, Mo. It illustrates the use of a light-duty truck as the basis for a Gatsby era wrecker.

Another Holmes 485 wrecker unit rides in the back of a Model AA Ford express truck donated by Connolly's Towing, of Arvada, Colorado. A big Weaver Auto Crane sits behind a second Model AA Ford truck that came from Bachman Towing Co., of Moundridge, Kansas. A converted '29 Chrysler passenger car, donated by O'Hare Truck Service, of Northlake, Illinois, carries a Weaver 3-ton Auto Crane.

Whealon Towing & Service, of Fond du Lac, Wisconsin, loaned the museum its red and white Chevrolet tow truck that carries a big Holmes 460 wrecker and 540-cradle combination. Another larger truck is a '40 GMC-produced COE model that carries lettering showing that it once worked for Lanser Garages and Towing, of Belgium, Wisconsin.

The Hall of Fame portion of the museum honors individuals who have, in various ways, significantly advanced the industry. Engineers, publicists, sales representatives, manufacturers, distributors and wrecker drivers are all honored. They come from the United States, as well as Australia, Canada, England, Germany, Japan, The Netherlands and South Africa.

Other memorabilia and artifacts related to the towing industry's colorful past also are also on display in showcases inside the nicely-restored brick building. They include collectible toys, tools, unique equipment and pictorial histories of manufacturers who have supplied the vintage equipment.

The International Towing and Recovery Hall of Fame and Museum is located at 3315 Broad St., Chattanooga, Tennessee 37408. Its regular hours are 10 a.m. - 4:30 p.m. weekdays, and 11 a.m. - 5 p.m. on weekends.

The collection offers extended hours during the summer, when tourist activity is at its peak. Admission is $8 ($7 for seniors and $4 for kids ages 5-18). Children under five are admitted free with adults. A gift shop sells souvenirs and other mementos related to the towing industry. For information and exact hours at a certain time of the year, call: (423) 267-3132.

The Ford Model AA truck of Bachman Towing, Moundridge, Kansas, was displayed at the International Towing and Recovery Museum. The Ford was equipped with a Weaver Auto Crane. (International Towing and Recovery Museum)

Bob Meyers Towing and Recovery supplied this Locomobile, outfitted with a Holmes 485 wrecker boom, to the International Towing and Recovery Hall of Fame in Chattanooga, Tennessee. (International Towing and Recovery Museum)

The distinctive-looking GMC COE tow truck of Lanser Garage and Towing, Inc., Belgium, Wisconsin, turned heads at the International Towing and Recovery Museum. (International Towing and Recovery Museum)

The International Towing and Recovery Museum takes its vehicles to shows for promotional purposes. Before World War II, used cars were converted for towing. This Chrysler-based tow car is owned by O'Hare Truck Service of Chicago, Illinois. (John Gunnell)

RESTORING THE '51 DODGE POWER WAGON

By Dave Netherland

I began working in the automobile business in 1949, for a Buick dealer in the Chicago suburbs. I worked nine hours a day, six days a week for 90 cents an hour. The labor rate charged by dealers at that time was $3.85 an hour. An enamel paint job cost $100 at that time and Duco lacquer paint jobs were $150. Restoring older vehicles back then was just a hobby, while today it's a big business for many people. I have always been interested in the restoration hobby.

I began working as the body shop manager at Dearth Motors in Monroe, Wisconsin, in 1982. Bob Dearth sold Chrysler Corporation cars and trucks. In 1951, Dearth Motors had purchased the Dodge Power-Wagon tow truck

that I restored after I retired. This truck held special sentimental value to my former boss. On Easter Sunday 1966, the city of Monroe had been hit by a tremendous tornado. Dearth Motors was leveled to the ground. The tow truck was the only thing that survived the storm and with only minor dings and scratches. All other vehicles inside and outside the devastated dealership building were so heavily damaged that they had to be sold to a salvage yard.

The dealership was rebuilt and the old Power-Wagon was kept as a memento of the original business. Eventually, it was stored in a metal building, with a cement floor, behind the dealership. This helped to preserve it. Periodically, it would be started and run for awhile, to keep

This is how the 1951 Dodge Power Wagon looked when Dave Netherland brought it home. He says he drove it at 35 to 40 mph "flat out," 20 to 25 mph going up hills and at 50 mph plus going downhill. (Dave Netherland)

the engine and drive train from freezing up.

From the time I started working for Dearth Motors, until my retirement in 1993, I had worked on building a shop in my back yard, so that I could do minor repairs and restorations. I had been doing such work for 43 years at that time and have added another decade of experience since my retirement. I still have five cars of my own to do. Then, I hope, I can retire for good.

Restoring the Dearth Motors tow truck was a great project, because it had been given good maintenance over the years. All the pieces were there and everything was operational. Bob Dearth also understood that restoring a vehicle today takes a lot of patience and discipline. A vehicle can be restored to "good enough" condition or better. Dearth wanted this one better.

I worked on the truck for a period of 14 months, taking it completely apart, stripping all the paint, sandblasting all rust, filling all pitted areas, straightening all dents and patch-repairing rust holes in the front fenders, running boards and brackets. The floor, doors and cab were solid and had no rust-through. Most of the glass was cracked or fogged around the edges, but a local glass house made new glass for us.

Although all the tow truck's parts were there, many components like the weather stripping and interior trim were worn. I found everything I needed through the *Old Cars Weekly* classified ads and Roberts Motor Parts.

The truck's old bed rail was in bad shape. A friend, who works as an electrician at a cheese factory, built a new bed rail. He fabricated it in two halves made out of stainless steel. We had trouble making the bends, as the metal tended to kink. To avoid this, we filled it with tightly-packed sand and wound up with perfect bends. We then used heli-arc welding to join the two pieces together. After smoothing the weld, we buffed it to a chrome-like sheen.

The Dodge engine was in excellent running condition. It was taken out of the truck and the manifolds were removed. Everything was degreased and sandblasted, with all openings taped over with duct tape to keep sand from getting inside. The engine was then sprayed with a high-temperature engine and manifold paint.

The cost of restoring the 1951 Dodge Power-Wagon tow truck was as follows:

Replacement parts including interior kit, nuts, bolts, clips, fasteners, a weather stripping kit, windshield, vent windows, rubber, four new inner tubes and other miscellaneous parts $2,575.56
Radiator repair and replace heater core. $184.00
Glass $255.40
Stainless steel bed rail $260.00
Lettering $335.00
Paint material $933.55
Chrome $200.00
Labor @ "don't bug me about when it's going to be done"
Rate of $20 per hour x 633 hours $12,660.00
Total 17,401.01

Restoration starts with disassembly. Fortunately, the old Dodge proved to be pretty solid. The main structure of the cab was very solid, but the doors had to come off. (Dave Netherland)

Before painting the cab's interior, the glass was removed and the steering wheel and steering column were masked with newspaper and tape. The floorboards were removed and painted separately. (Dave Netherland)

All parts, like the doors, hood and wrecker crane seen here, were taken off the Dodge and sandblasted down to bare metal. Small amounts of rust holes were patched. (Dave Netherland)

Here's a shot of the tow crane assembly, sandblasted down to bare metal. Working alone, Dave used this framed stand to hold the tow assembly after sliding it from the tow body of the truck. (Dave Netherland)

Smaller parts, like headlamp components, as well as the front fenders, were removed and restored one by one. The lower front fenders were rusted and had to be repaired with metal patches. (Dave Netherland)

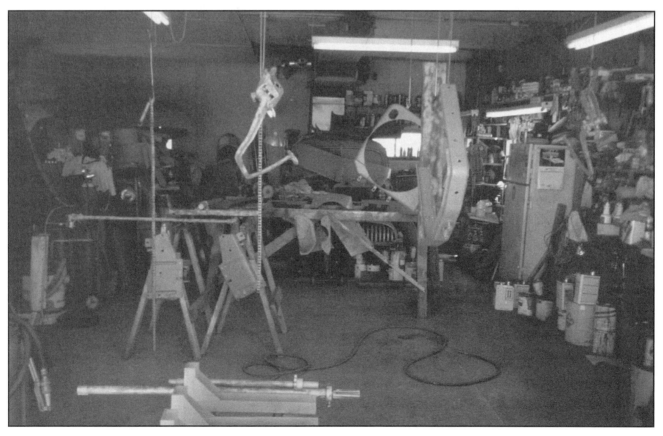

While some parts were hung up for sandblasting and priming, parts like the running board brackets, lower left, were fabricated by Dave to save money. (Dave Netherland)

After being removed, sandblasted, and repaired as needed, the hood was primed and then given a top coat of paint. The hood and other parts were suspended to dry. (Dave Netherland)

The doors hang from the ceiling after being painted. Restoration takes a lot of space and supplies to be done successfully. (Dave Netherland)

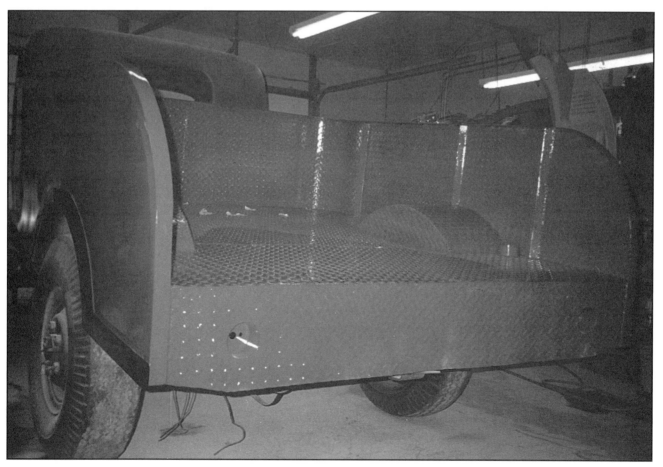

The taillights were moved from the crane assembly to the lower bed skirting. The diamond-plate metal bed was completely refinished while the crane assembly was off. (Dave Netherland)

The tow crane assembly was sandblasted, primer coated and then was given a fresh coat of bright red paint to make it look new again. (Dave Netherland)

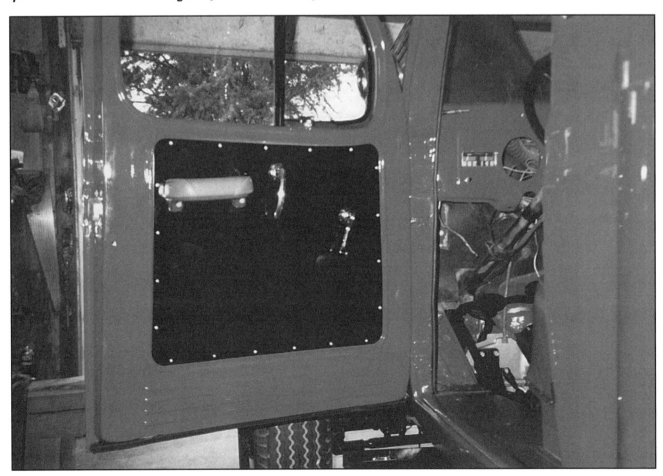

Interior details were considered too. Dave found the interior door trim parts he needed through ads in Old Cars Weekly and through Roberts Motor Parts, a Mopar vendor. (Dave Netherland)

The engine was in good condition and needed the manifold removed for cleaning and painting silver. The engine has black accessories. (Dave Netherland)

Hoisting the hoist! Dave used a come-along and large bracing to fashion a hoist to lift the wrecking crane back into the Dodge's bed. The truck lacks glass and others parts. (Dave Netherland)

Nearing final stages of restoration, the Dodge Power Wagon still lacks glass, its hood and fenders as well as bumpers, accessories and paint detailing. (Dave Netherland)

After being repaired for rust damage and primer coated, the fenders were given a shiny black coat and set across wooden saw horses to dry. (Dave Netherland)

Here's a rear view of the nearly restored Dodge Power Wagon tow truck. Cardboard sheets and towels help guard the surfaces from scratches. Lights were re-mounted. (Dave Netherland)

Dave's careful restoration looked this way the day he returned it to Dearth Motors. It was completely redone and was ready for graphics and other lettering. (Dave Netherland)

Rehburger Stands For Rare
By Tom Collins

"One of a kind" often is an overused phrase. In this case, this 1926 Rehburger tow truck is a one of a kind.

If you lived outside the Newark, New Jersey, area after 1938, you may never have heard of a Rehburger truck. Arthur Rehburger and Sons produced 1 1/2- to 7-ton trucks in limited numbers between 1923 and 1938. In 1933, the height of the Great Depression, the company switched to bus chassis production.

The Rehburger trucks went out of production just prior to WWII but the company survived a few more years building trailers for the U.S. Navy and for shipbuilders during the war years. They failed to resurrect post-war truck building plans.

This mint Rehburger recently sold at a 2003 Kruse auction of collector Don Dougherty's vehicles in California for $25,000. The only one known to exist, it carries serial number 148, one of the few ever produced in the Newark assembly plant.

Powered by a four-cylinder Buda engine, it rides on Shuler front axles and a Timkin rear axle. The transmission is a Fuller with a two-plate clutch, similar to modern truck clutches.

On the working end is a Manley crane from the 1920s. Manley tow cranes were made in York, Pennsylvania. Like modern tow trucks, the Rehburger has a spotlight mounted for night duty.

The standard features on this Rehburger included an enclosed "C"-shaped cab with ventilated windshield, front fenders, running boards, a Dot lubrication system and taillights. It has cowl mounted headlights and carries a special tool kit. Note the antique Texaco oil can on the running board.

No "flapper" in distress or playboy driving his Jordan, Stutz or Kissel "Gold Bug" speedster ever got into enough danger to deter the Rehburger tow truck from coming to the rescue. It's a unique reminder of towing's past, now more than 75 years young.

The Manley tow crane looks ready to hook up to double-barreled action. Manley was an early manufacturer of tow equipment and was based in York, Pennsylvania. (Ron Kowalke)

A VERY RELIABLE PARING   *By Tom Collins*

Donal Loker of Penn Laird, Virginia, in the beautiful Shenandoah Valley, has seen many tow trucks since he began driving one at age 19 in 1960. He started towing with a '49 Ford F-600 that carried a National hand crane.

Today, his son, Keith, carries on Penn Laird Towing—a business that features a range of towing services and a fleet of versatile trucks. Donal enjoys collecting and restoring older tow trucks. One is very special, a 1920 Model T Ford coupled with a 1920 Reliable tow crane.

The venerable Ford Model T is one of the world's best known vehicles. Millions of the "Tin Lizzies" were a common sight on roads in every corner of the globe before Ford ended production in 1927.

Much rarer is the Reliable tow equipment. Reliable was a product of Elite Manufacturing of Ashland, Ohio. Elite began making Reliable tools for auto repair in 1906. Along the way, they added tow cranes to their product line that included hoists, jacks, stands and more.

In his 1989 book "The World History of the Towing and Recovering Industry," author John L. Hawkins II mentions a lone Reliable example that had surfaced at the time. It was fitted to a handsome Ford owned by Kent Garvin of Mankato, Minnesota.

Like the Model T, the Reliable crane represents an original. It is a rare and treasured example of an era when the towing industry was just beginning.

Donal Loker of Penn Laird, Virginia, owns this rare 1920 Reliable tow unit mounted on a 1920 Model T Ford. Reliable equipment was made in Ashland, Ohio. (Donal Loker)

Donal has several trucks he purchased new and kept or chose to restore. His historic fleet includes a 1932 Ford coupled with a Holmes 110 crane and a '34 Ford with a Weaver unit. He says his 1946 Ford COE always draws attention. Donal's trucks offer a glimpse of towing's past.

Vehicles like the Model T and cranes like the Reliable pioneered the towing industry. A reliable pairing that set the standard for all that followed.

The 1948 Ford COE with Sasgen Derrick tow unit looks like it's brand new. The Ford is part of a collection owned by Donal Loker of Penn Laird, Virginia. (Donal Loker)

Suddenly it's 1952 Again!

By Tom Collins

For John Murray of La Mirada, California, 1952 means more than the premier of "Today" or "I Love Lucy" on TV, the election of former Gen. Dwight Eisenhower as President of the United States or the Lions and Red Wings bringing championships to Detroit.

It was John's favorite year for the cars he enjoys, so he remembers it in a unique way. He collects 1952 Fords!

He owns two Ford convertibles plus a Victoria and a sedan delivery. He thought he'd add a tow truck to the Murray '52 Ford "fleet."

His investment of $499.99 on the Internet bought his '52 Ford F-4 tow truck, direct from an Iowa farm where it had sat unused for 30 years.

"When the owner opened the door, he said 1,000 mice came out," says John. "They were even in the clutch and pressure plate!"

While the Ford was missing the upper portions of its engine and had no radiator, the towing end was intact. John says the diamond plate wasn't even rusty.

He replaced the front end with parts from a '52 Ford stake truck. John worked on his F-4 at Cerritos College where he was taking auto body classes.

"It took about three years to complete the restoration," he says. "Last car show I went to, I got first place in the commercial class."

John replaced what was left of the original engine with a '52 Ford 215-cid ohv six-cylinder power plant and a four-speed spur transmission. The 3-ton Ford has dual rear wheels and a 5.14 rear axle. The Ford's working tow unit is a rare Sasgen Derrick made in Chicago, Illinois.

"Only the Sasgen gives you the advantage of patented Adjustable Circle Swing Boom which can turn a full 360 degrees," claimed the company's ad in the 1952 Hildy's Blue Book, the Ford truck special equipment catalog.

"Get easier, speedier lifting with Sasgen Derricks. [The operator] can stand right on the truck when operating the derrick, because gearing is high on the mast! No need to get down in the mud or on a slippery road," explained the Sasgen ad.

Some may remember 1952 for Maureen "Little Mo" Connelly, the Wimbledon and U.S. Open champion as a teen, or the Olympics in Helsinki, Finland, or even the premier of "Mr. Peepers" with Wally Cox.

John Murray enjoys riding in his 1952 Fords, including his F-4 Ford tow truck with the Sasgen Derrick. John and his Fords have made 1952 a year to remember!

John Murray's red and white tow truck shines in the California sun. He bought it from an Iowa farm where it had sat dormant for over 30 years. (John Murray)

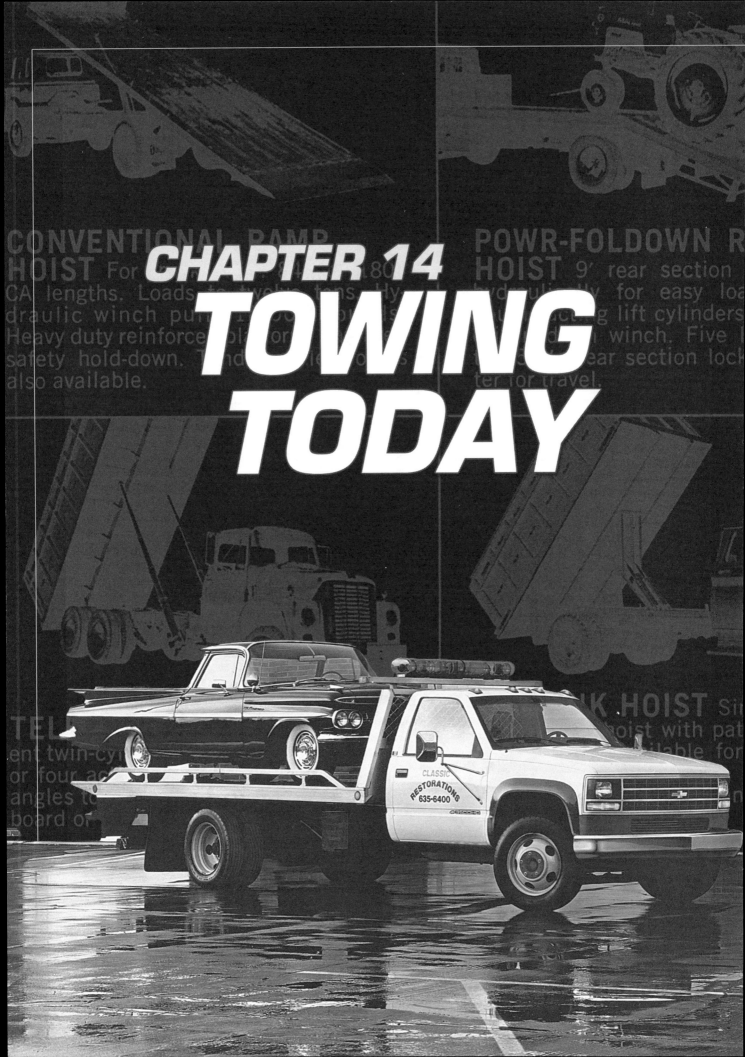

CHAPTER 14
TOWING TODAY

FLAT TOWS

By John Gunnell

"Flat toes" does not refer to something you have to make an appointment to see a podiatrist for. Flat-bed, ramp-style, tilt-bed and bend-in-the-middle towing might seem like the latest thing to some people who associate boom-and-crane type wreckers with the early days of towing cars. However, as the accompanying photos show, there were flat-towing alternatives way back when.

The fellow wearing a cadet-style cap and coveralls is hauling that old car with no rear wheels on his flatbed. The truck appears to be a Model T Ford with a chassis extension and a homemade wooden platform. The roadster atop the truck is a Chevrolet and the picture dates from around 1920 or earlier. Though no competition for Jerr-Dan, these guys were ahead of their time.

There's something scary about hauling a speedy racing car around on a beer truck, but that was the Indy 500 back in the '30s. The wooden crates hold Edelweiss lager and the

A 1920s photo of a Model T flatbed hauling a Chevy roadster lacking rear wheels. (OCW)

A 1929 or '30 Chevrolet truck carried the Edelweiss Special race car to the Indianapolis Motor Speedway in 1933. (IMSC)

lettering on the side of the crates describes them as "A case of good judgment." Hopefully, the guy in the cab was using a bit of the same, and staying away from the suds when he was driving.

The flat bed truck hauling the beer is a 1929 or 1930 Chevy and the cargo deck is low enough to the ground that loading the "Edelweiss Special" race car was probably a snap. The sideboards slide into metal brackets and keep the car — and beer — from racing off.

Conventional and Rollback Ramp Hoist trucks started to appear in the late '60s, along with power fold-down ramp hoist. A 1969 advertisement from *The Chevrolet Silver Book* (a catalog of so-called "vocational" bodies engineered for Chevrolet trucks), showed such models made by E.R. Schwartz Co. of Lester Prairie, Minn. That same year, Leland Equipment Co. of Oklahoma City, showed several low-loader trailer models in the same Silver Book.

The popularity of flat tow trucks continued to grow throughout the '70s, '80s and '90s, and many technological advances were made. In a 1991 publicity photo, Chevrolet depicted a roll-back tow body on its C3500 HD (heavy-duty with tandem rear wheels) 1-ton truck chassis. It

showed the name Classic Restorations on the side and was depicted hauling a fully-restored '59 El Camino.

The idea of a new Chevy truck hauling an old one gets a collector's juices flowing and Studebaker fanatics are no different. Although Studebaker built some very nice trucks, the 1950s model, pictured on page 198, wasn't built at the factory with the roll-back bed that's carrying a classic Studebaker Starlight coupe. Nevertheless, it makes a great combination for traveling to old-car shows.

Another thing you see a lot of at car shows and auctions is slant-back tow trucks hauling collector-cars and trucks. Many restoration shops, dealers and private enthusiasts now own car haulers.

Car haulers and flat tow trucks also have great appeal to racers who can't quite afford their own semi-type transporter and rolling machine shop. So, it's no wonder a talented modeler made a miniature of a Pennsylvania car dealer's race rig, complete with a scaled-down Holmes tilt-back tow truck. It's a beauty, down to its realistic E/H mud flaps and we think it belongs in the International Towing & Recovery Museum's collection of toy tow trucks.

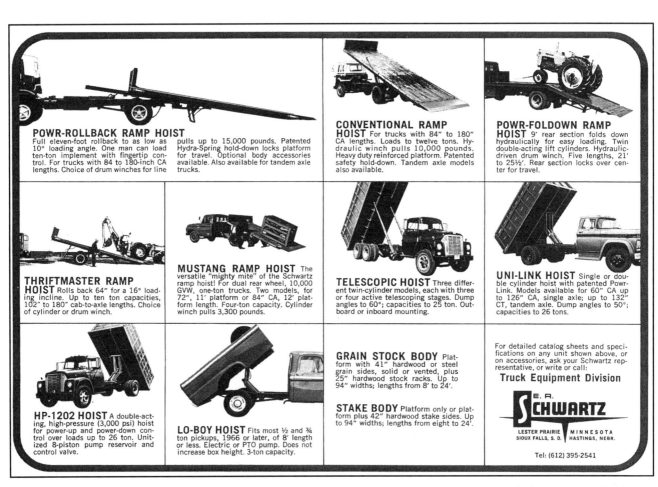

In 1969, E. R. Schwartz, an approved truck equipment maker for Chevrolet, offered five types of fold-down or rollback hoists for Chevrolet chassis. (John Gunnell)

Leland Equipment Co. turned out a variety of trailers that a tow service could make good use of back in 1969. (John Gunnell)

A rollback tow body on a *1991 Chevy one-ton hauls a restored 1959 El Camino, the first year those vehi-cles were produced.* (Chevrolet Motors Division)

A Studebaker fan made his personalized rollback to haul his white Studebaker Starlight coupe. (OCW)

A 1998 Chevrolet C3500 HD chassis-and-cab with rollback body hauls a customized 1958 Chevrolet 3100 Apache Stepside pickup. (Chevrolet Motors Division)

A modeler made this miniature Chevrolet with a Holmes rollback unit to carry a replica of the Hiram Wible and Son racing car. (OCW)

CAR-PULL TUNNEL TRUCKS

By John Gunnell

In the trade, they call them "custom tunnel wreckers." They are specially designed to pull damaged or disabled cars out of the narrow tunnels that surround major cities like New York and Baltimore. They usually carry an assortment of special accessories and equipment to help them accomplish that demanding job, as well as other problems that could pop up in the underground environment.

According to company president Joseph Milan, Weld Built Body Co., of Wyandanch, New York, has been supplying such trucks for 45 years. The firm's customers have included the Port Authority Trans Hudson (known as "PATH" in New York and New Jersey), the Maryland Transportation Authority, the Chesapeake Bay Bridge and Tunnel District, the Virginia Department of Transportation, the New York City Triborough Bridge and Tunnel Authority, the Colorado Department of Transportation and the Kentucky Cumberland Gap Tunnel Authority.

The typical tunnel wrecker is a powerful, compact vehicle specifically designed to rapidly clear narrow and congested bridges and tunnels of disabled vehicles. A heavy-duty cab-over-engine truck is modified for mounting on a special short-wheelbase chassis. The wrecker bodies are completely custom built, as is a sturdy towing boom that can drag anything from a Mazda to a Mack truck out of a tunnel.

In addition to ordinary towing accessories like push plates, winches and lights, custom tunnel wreckers are often required to carry firefighting equipment, in case a damaged vehicle starts burning underground.

Models such as Weld Built's "Tunnel Sentry" — a 20-ton capacity hydraulic tunnel wrecker with a 98-inch wheelbase — have a retracted-boom rating of 40,000 pounds and a tow rating of 80,000 pounds. With twin 8,000-pound front hydraulic winches and 30,000-pound rear upright hydraulic winches, the Sentry is suitable for towing buses and semi-trailer trucks, as well as any type of car.

Other standard features of the Sentry include 75 feet of 5/8-inch cable on each drum, winch cable tensioners, a non-telescopic reinforced box boom, a custom body with 1-1/4-inch thick front and rear plates for counter-balance, side tool compartments with aluminum roll-up doors, interior compartment lighting, dual rear control stations with kill switches, a custom highlight pylon, a glad hand and trailer plug connectors, federal light package No. 108, a super-duty tow bar with rubber rings, a hydraulic PTO and

The front view of a 1990s-style tunnel tow truck with a Weld Built body. This truck features a yellow finish with red stripes and it may have been for the New York Port Authority's civilian drivers. (Weld Built Body Co.)

pump and a safety chain and hook-up package.

Factory options that Weld Built supplies for this model start with a rear under-lift apparatus complete with remote control, automobile wheel lift attachments, frame forks and removable pintle hooks (6,500-10,000-pound lift capacity models are available). In addition, Weld Built offers firefighting apparatus, hydraulic vertical rear body jacks, automobile tow sling assemblies with chains, spotlights, work lights, Karstarts, bar lights, snatch blocks, wheel chocks, painting options and aluminum décor packages.

In the 1970s, Weld Built manufactured a fleet of three custom tunnel trucks for use in Baltimore's Ft. McHenry Tunnel, which handled 85,000 vehicles a day at that time. These trucks cost $133,000 each and the sale to the State of Maryland was made by Chesapeake Truck Sales, a veteran heavy-duty truck dealer in the Baltimore area. June Kleeman, the dealership's vice president of marketing noted, "Because of the exacting equipment specifications and the need for vehicles capable of exceptional maneuverability within the narrow tunnel, this was a very difficult contract to win."

The trucks were Freightliner FLT6342 cab-over-engine tractors with 330-hp Detroit Diesel engines and Allison HT-750 DR transmissions. All components on these units were custom specified. The specs called for Rockwell FF-941 front axles, Eaton 23121 rear axles (with a 4.56:1 gear ratio) and Michelin 16-ply low-profile tires. These trucks had a 111-inch wheelbase that helped them make tight turns in 22-foot wide, two-lane sections of the tunnel.

Freightliner offered to build the trucks to be short enough to meet the state's specifications and the Weld Built wrecker bodies were specially-designed to fit the Freightliner chassis-and-cab units. They were equipped with a 10-ton capacity rear hoist and a 3-ton recessed front hydraulic hoist. Each truck carried twin 16-ton wrecker booms and twin 16,000-pound rear-mounted Braden winches. Up front were two 8,000-pound winches, also sourced from Braden. The trucks were equipped with firefighting equipment, including a 300-gallon water tank located immediately behind the cab.

In New York, PATH had operated a fleet of International tunnel wreckers with Weld Built bodies. These trucks had a 99-inch wheelbase and an overall length of 14-1/2 feet. In 1986, PATH designed a new model and Weld Built turned out 16 or 17 of these custom tunnel wreckers to replace the old Internationals. They were mounted on a 48,000-pound capacity Mack truck chassis. Power came from a 230-hp diesel engine driving through an Allison automatic transmission. Their all-hydraulic wrecker bodies featured two 20,000-pound rear hoists that could perform stationary lifts in excess of 40,000 pounds.

Some of the trucks were operated by PATH police officers who had special training as tow truck operators and others had civilian drivers.

According to labor union contract rules, the trucks manned by police officers are painted white with blue stripes, while the civilian units are finished in yellow. Tunnel wreckers from the 1990s and 2000s haven't changed drastically from the 1986 versions, but have slightly more modern-looking cabs.

Strong, maneuverable and compact, Weld Built's Port Authority tow truck is designed for emergency operations in tight quarters. This police unit rides on a Mack chassis. (Weld Built Body Co.)

With power and muscle in a compact tow/ emergency truck, this Mack and Weld Built combination serves the famed Port Authority police of New York and New Jersey. (Weld Built Body Co.)

The Weld Built name is carried on both the rear fender and mud flaps of this truck. These specially built tunnel trucks can handle just about any rush-hour emergency. (Weld Built Body Co.)

JERR-DAN PIONEERED THE ROLLBACK

By John Gunnell

"Looking back over the years, I can see growth and evolution into a much larger and more diverse company than was here in the 1970s."

So said Jerrey Weller, president of Jerr-Dan Corporation, in 2002. That was the year the Greencastle, Pennsylvania tow truck manufacturer celebrated its 30th anniversary. The company produces both conventional wreckers that pull cars behind them and rollback carriers used for flat tows.

Jerr-Dan was formed in 1972 and always has operated at the same location. Its ads claim the company has "the guts to get it done." A reputation for pioneering technological advancements has helped the firm build that gutsy image.

"Design innovation was present when we pioneered the rollback carrier in the 1970s," Weller explained. "And each new product (since then) has produced a higher level of customer satisfaction."

Rollback tow trucks feature a flat platform that rides downward on rollers, turning it into a ramp that the car can be driven aboard or pulled up on. The hydraulically-operated platform then moves back up the rollers and levels off, so the vehicle being towed rides flat on the back of the truck.

Jerr-Dan evolved from a firm named Grove Manufacturing that developed rollback truck technology in the 1960s. Grove's first rollback was called the Super Series, a trade name still used by Jerr-Dan today. The Super Series was designed for delivering farm equipment to dealers. The earliest carrier bodies were constructed of heavy-gauge steel and rode on steel rollers. They soon were nicknamed "rollbacks."

For farm equipment and forklift transportation, the early Super Series' heavy-gauge steel construction was a necessity. It was well suited to handling such large, heavy machines.

In 1977, Jerr-Dan entered the automobile-transportation industry when it brought out a new lightweight truck body called the Aluminum Wrangler. This rollback unit was light enough to be installed on 1-ton chassis-and-cab trucks, which made it much more practical and affordable for tow service operators who wanted to haul mostly cars and light trucks.

In 1982, Jerr-Dan introduced a new rollback carrier called the Wrangler Lite. It featured an extruded aluminum body that made it even lighter than the Aluminum Wrangler. As cars grew smaller, the Aluminum Wrangler found a larger market.

It was about this time that front-wheel-drive cars started booming in popularity in the United States. Rollback carriers were particularly well-suited for hauling such vehicles. As automobile design trends moved more in both directions, the rollback carrier suddenly became a necessary part of every commercial tow truck fleet.

The 1980s marked another period of strong growth for Jerr-Dan Corporation. The company started to expand the distribution of its growing line of car carriers geographically, selling them through independent distributors throughout the country. In 1985, the firm introduced the industry's first tow truck featuring a modular-aluminum body.

In 1987, Jerr-Dan expanded into the vehicle-recovery market with a new line of HPL light-duty wreckers. These trucks sported 60- to 84-inch CA modular-aluminum bodies and came with a choice of single- or dual-line winches.

In 1990, the LP8500 Shark was introduced. This new carrier body utilized a patented dual-angle deck design with the industry's lowest load angle.

A Jerr-Dan distribution facility opened in Las Vegas, Nevada, in 1994. It handled distributor stocking throughout the Western United states.

In 1995, Jerr-Dan entered the heavy-duty wrecker market. By 1996, it had pioneered another industry first – the composite body. Through the end of the '90s and into the new millennium, Jerr-Dan added 14-, 16-, 25- 30-, 35- and 55-ton composite-body wreckers.

At Jerr-Dan, the manufacturing process has kept pace with new-product introductions. A state-of-the-art dedicated wrecker plant was built just a mile from the company's original site.

It opened in July 1996. The original manufacturing plant was also expanded and converted into a factory that built only rollback carriers.

Both of the company's plants feature the latest manufacturing assembly and finishing technologies — the same used in the automotive industry. They employ automated paint systems, plasma cutters, high-tech materials, robotic welding and "rhythmical" assembly methods.

In 2002, Jerr-Dan introduced a product called the Self-Loader. Unveiled at the 2002 Professional Wrecker Operators of Florida (PWOF) tow show in Florida, the unit's Quick-Pick moves and lifts from uneven ground using two unique design features: a 10-degree negative down tilt and true 90-degree lifting.

NEW IDEA: ROADSIDE ASSISTANCE, FLATBEDS TOWING FOR COLLECTORS

By John Gunnell

The Hagerty insurance company of Traverse City, Michigan, always has been an innovator, first insuring classic boats and later offering similar low-cost coverage to vintage car collectors. Late in 2002, the firm, known for its aggressive and witty advertising campaigns, launched the first-ever "roadside assistance program" for those who collect classic cars. The plan includes a variety of services and up to three free flatbed tows per year to members who break down or have an accident with their specialty vehicle.

Teresa Leach, director of Hagerty's Special Account Services, said the program was being offered to new and existing customers who buy their specialty insurance through the company. It was designed to help car collectors better protect their vehicles and enjoy them more.

Coach-Net/National Motor Club of America was contacted to provide 24-hour, seven-days-a-week flatbed towing service exclusively for those who became members of the program. The service was made available anywhere in the U.S. and Canada. Coach-Net, based in Lake Havasu City, Arizona, already specialized in providing automotive emergency assistance and technical support to RV owners.

A Peterbilt and modern flatbed hauls this beautiful blue 1959 Cadillac convertible. (Hagerty Insurance Co.)

Flatbed towing is a safer and more secure method for transporting classic and vintage cars because it affords maximum protection for undercarriages, body work and paint finish.

Hagerty's research indicates collector car owners are six times more likely to suffer mechanical breakdowns, battery failures or flat tires and require vehicle towing, than they are to file an insurance damage claim. The Roadside Assistance program includes services for a mechanical breakdown so a vehicle may drive or be towed to a service provider to repair a problem.

Services available through the roadside assistance program include up to three roadside calls per year (up to $50 per incident), adjustments from a mobile mechanic to enable the vehicle to operate under its own power or be towed to the nearest qualified repair facility, battery jump starts (or delivery of a new battery), tire service (to install an inflated spare or deliver a replacement tire), fuel delivery (if the vehicle runs out of gas) and lock-out service, including assistance to replace lost keys. Parts such as new batteries, tires, fuel and mechanical labor are additional.

In addition to the roadside assistance benefits, plan members will get a quarterly newsletter, online policy management services, access to a members-only Website and Hagerty's commitment to protect their member interests through hobby advocacy and legislative watchdog programs.

Information about the program is available by calling 1-800-922-4050 or by visiting www.hagerty.com.

A flatbed tow truck hauls a classic Corvette. Both the truck and Corvette stand out in the desert setting. (Hagerty Insurance Co.)

Knights (and Ladies) Keep Australia's "Truckies" Out of Trouble
By Tom Collins

Drivers have something in common all over the world. Their cars or trucks get into accidents or have breakdowns.

Few places on earth are as isolated for drivers as Australia's Outback.

There, "truckies" drive their "pri-movers" that pull up to three 44-foot trailers filled with every kind of cargo and weighing 115 tons. Adelaide tow truck driver Kingsley Foreman helps keep them running.

"Most of Australia's pri-movers are Macks and Kenworths that run 500 or 600 hp engines and have, at minimum, a 13-speed gear box. Chassis are stronger, the trucks have air tanks for tire inflation and extra fuel tanks to deal with 1,000 mile or longer trips."

"Truckies have to be mechanically inclined and able to make repairs to a broken-down rig," he adds. "If the truckie cannot fix the problem, he or she will have to wait for someone to come out hundreds of miles to get the truck going again."

Australian tow trucks serving the Outback have to be specially prepared to drive the same distances and must be able to tow 120 tons—the entire road train load.

"If a rig blows a motor or gearbox, there's no alternative but to get towed. It is not unusual for the road-train to be towed hundreds of miles to the nearest town, where the trailers are unhooked before the rig is then towed additional hundreds of miles to a city in the southern part of Australia to be fixed."

Originally, Australian road trains were made up of six to eight 20-foot trailers towed by military surplus Army trucks that had no air brake systems. They inched forward slowly to gain a speed of 30 mph and had to coast to a stop.

Kangaroos and free-roaming cattle can cause havoc for pri-mover and tow truck drivers cruising along at 65 mph. Sudden stops are too dangerous, so Australians use aluminum or steel "bull bar" cages on the front to protect their rigs from damage.

"It's not unusual to hit four or five kangaroos on one trip," Kingsley says.

Bull bars can cost as much as $2,000 Australian but he says that's far cheaper than paying for a new front end.

Kingsley says Australian tow drivers who deal with road trains like to use traditional Garwood tow cranes mounted on a shorter wheelbase truck chassis.

"If you use a modern under lifter, the long wheel base you need makes it hard to get around the rough of road accident scenes. Plus so many of our trucks have the big bull bars so you can hook them up from the front without doing any damage."

No matter where the breakdown might be, a helpful "towie" will be dispatched, often as far as 700 miles. The vehicle is serviced to run again or is prepared for what Aussies call "smash repairs."

These knights and ladies of the highways do such a good job that they've been recognized publicly. United Towing, a firm that serves Victoria state, was the first towing company to receive Australia's prestigious Standard of Quality certification—high praise for any business.

American tow operators traveling in Australia, Europe or elsewhere would recognize the "business end" of tow vehicles, too. Manufacturers like Holmes, Jerr-Dan, Challenger and others have operations as well known in Adelaide as they are in Abilene.

The next time you see a stranded motorist or truck driver, remember the man or woman dispatched to help is trying to be part of the solution. Help will be on the way.

In Australia, the knights and ladies who come to serve "truckies" and others will be what they like to call a "dinkum towie."

A W model Kenworth brings back what appears to be a damaged International C-O Transtar hauling sand or lime. It was hit by a car traveling in the wrong lane. Right-hand drive in Australia means the "truckie" felt the brunt of the collision. (Kingsley Foreman)

Our Thanks

In appreciation of the dedicated men and women, tow truck drivers around the world, who keep our wheels rolling and save us from danger.